The Art of Edward Thomas

Edward Thomas in the Artists' Rifles

The Art of Edward Thomas

Edited & Introduced by
Jonathan Barker

POETRY WALES PRESS
1987

POETRY WALES PRESS
56 PARCAU AVENUE, BRIDGEND, MID GLAMORGAN

British Library Cataloguing in Publication Data

The Art of Edward Thomas
1. Thomas, Edward, *1878-1917* — Criticism and interpretation
I. Barker, Jonathan, *1949-*
821'.912 PR6039.H55Z/

ISBN 0-907476-66-X

Cover Design: Jeane Rees

Frontispiece by kind permission of Mrs Myfanwy Thomas

Published with the financial support of the
Welsh Arts Council

Printed in 10 point Baskerville by
The Camelot Press plc, Southampton

Contents

Acknowledgements

I would like to thank Cary Archard and Mick Felton of Poetry Wales Press for their involvement in the production of this book. Also R. George Thomas, Myfanwy Thomas and the Oxford University Press for permission to quote from *The Collected Poems of Edward Thomas* edited and introduced by R. George Thomas (1978). I am grateful to the following libraries for providing books by and on the subject: the Arts Council Poetry Library, the Library at Cecil Sharp House, the British Library, Reference Division, and especially the University of London Library, Senate House. But most of all to my wife Deirdre for making Edward Thomas a most welcome guest in our home so soon after the departure of his friend W.H. Davies.

Introduction

Poetry readers have kept the poems of Edward Thomas in print for at least the past fifty years and those poems are today more read, written on and studied than ever before. Other poets especially have always appreciated him and written poems in tribute, from contemporaries such as Robert Frost, Walter De La Mare, W.H. Davies, Ivor Gurney, Gordon Bottomley, to Alun Lewis and many poets of our day who continue to pay tribute in poems and prose, among them Philip Larkin, R.S. Thomas, James Wright, Andrew Motion, Tom Paulin, Dannie Abse, Michael Longley and the poets who write in this book. The events of Thomas's life and writing are included in the Chronology and Bibliography on page 11 but it is worth noting here, as contributors to this book point out, that his first prose book *The Woodland Life* was published in 1897 at the age of nineteen; within three years he was living by his pen producing eventually over thirty prose books; that he edited over a dozen others, and wrote over a thousand reviews containing one million words in all. He met Robert Frost, a fellow spirit in detachment and intensity, late in 1913 and, between December 1914 and January 1917 he wrote all of the one hundred and forty-four poems in *The Collected Poems of Edward Thomas* (1978). *Poems* was posthumously published six months after Thomas's death at Arras in April, 1917; followed by *Last Poems* in 1918.

Thomas's popularity with poets and poetry readers has, until quite recently, been matched by a more or less general lack of critical attention from all but converted enthusiasts. A fact bound up with the view that, although none of his poems appeared in Edward Marsh's popular *Georgian Poetry* anthologies published between 1912 and 1922, Thomas has too often been erroneously labelled a 'Georgian', a term upon which much critical abuse has been heaped by those who assume that what is popular *has* to be bad. Literary critics for decades assumed that Modernism was the only twentieth-century literary movement deserving much attention; a hypothesis which encouraged worthy exegesis on T.S. Eliot and latterly Ezra Pound, while simultaneously passing over Thomas Hardy, A.E. Housman, Edward Thomas, and Ivor Gurney. The past fourteen years have seen a steady retreat from this untenable position, and with it these poets have tardily joined the canon. Moreover a new generation of critics have come to see the old divisions between Modernist and native traditions as increasingly irrelevant, and a barrier to the proper appreciation of good writing of any kind. *Prufrock and Other Observations* was published just two months after Thomas's death: might he have valued the new voice as he did that of Ezra Pound in a review of *Personae* in 1909, or Robert Frost's 'revolutionary' *North of Boston* of 1914? Possibly not, but either way, the isolation and internal questioning, the sensibility of modern man are expressed variously by both Eliot and Thomas, in their very different ways poets alike of the difficulties and complexities of living. The young W.H. Auden for one certainly found no problem in being equally attracted by Thomas Hardy, Edward Thomas and T.S. Eliot: each understood the correlation between the dark and light of life, which in Thomas's own work appears in his twin themes of delight and melancholy. Jesse Berridge's memoir (in *The Letters of Edward Thomas to Jesse Berridge*, Enitharmon Press, 1983) acknowledges both sides of his friend, but deprecates "over-emphasis on the darker side of his unique personality": he records how Thomas could change from the "depths of depression" and anxiety, swinging "quickly to an almost boisterous hilarity over a song that we both knew, of dubious decency...". Berridge also comments that Thomas's "sense of the ridiculous often approached hysteria to my sober view, and it was very catching", a point worth remembering when we take too seriously the rather theatrical suicidal journal entry quoted on page 141 of R. George Thomas's *Edward Thomas: A Portrait* (Oxford University Press, 1985).

One of the first published critics of Edward Thomas was Walter De La Mare, who, in October 1917, wrote in the *Times Literary Supplement* of his "poetry that not only breaks away from poetic convention, into a verse in which the rhymes are the faintest of echoes, the metre at times scarcely distinguishable, and the form as insubstantial as a ghost's, but much of it is 'about' what most poets leave unremarked, or, at any rate, unrecorded". Other early admirers include John Middleton Murry, and Edgell Rickword who, in 1920, wrote in the *Daily Herald*, "there was surely never a poet so direct, so free from hyperbole and periphrase as Edward Thomas. To read him is like listening to a friend in the completest intimacy...". F.R. Leavis's *New Bearings in English Poetry* (1932) praised Thomas's "quiet, ruminative speech" and the "fidelity with which Thomas records the modern disintegration, the sense of directionlessness". In 1936 Michael Roberts chose to exclude Thomas Hardy and Edward Thomas from his influential *The Faber Book of Modern Verse*, perhaps still the most impressive anthology of the period, and one that did much to shape public taste. Critical neglect unfortunately put the onus on those who wrote on Thomas to argue his case against the mainstream. Nonetheless important contributions to the study of Thomas have been made by a number of enthusiastic biographers and critics. First was R.P. Eckert's *Edward Thomas: A Biography and a Bibliography* (1937), followed by John Moore's *The Life and Letters of Edward Thomas*

(1939), H. Coombes's *Edward Thomas: A Critical Study* (1956), C. Day Lewis's essay included in *Essays by Divers Hands* (1956), Philip Hobsbaum's essay of 1961 reprinted in *Twentieth Century Poetry: Critical Essays and Documents* ed. Graham Martin & P.N. Furbank (1975), and Vernon Scannell's British Council Writers and Their Work booklet of 1962. William Cooke's *Edward Thomas: A Critical Biography 1878-1917* (1970) is an important source of biographical, bibliographical and critical information, and C.H. Sisson's *English Poetry 1900-1950* (1971) argues well for Thomas. Edna Longley's exhaustive annotations to her edition of *Poems and Last Poems* (1973) were an important contribution, later complemented by *A language not to be betrayed* (1981), a selection of Thomas's prose, and two important essays in *Poetry in the Wars* (1986). But most of all we should be grateful for R. George Thomas's scholarly edition of *The Collected Poems of Edward Thomas* (Oxford University Press, 1978) providing the definitive text, and his official biography *Edward Thomas: A Portrait* (Oxford University Press, 1985) providing much new biographical information used by contributors to the present anthology. Two other useful studies are Jan Marsh's *Edward Thomas: A Poet for his Country* (1978) and Andrew Motion's *The Poetry of Edward Thomas* (1980). New books by Stan Smith and Michael Kirkham appeared in 1986.

But there has been dissent too. Donald Davie's *Thomas Hardy and British Poetry* (1973) for the first time examined the contemporary influence of Hardy seriously; although it puzzled many by its total exclusion of all comment on Thomas. A point of view perhaps explained in Davie's important lengthy review in the *Times Literary Supplement* of November 23rd 1979, where he expressed a generally dim view of Thomas criticism: "No one has yet made a case for Edward Thomas that doesn't sound like special pleading", while concluding "the least we can do as his centenary passes is to declare that in him we gave a great poet to the world, or at least to the English-speaking world". Davie's rigorous critical attitude, rejecting what he saw as a tendency to treat Thomas "as an insular speciality, to be taken out and caressed only when no troublesome strangers are about", and therefore somehow beyond the bounds of normal textual examination, was timely. It brought out into the open the approach of wholly arguing *for* Thomas which I think the Modernist critical orthodoxy forced on those who liked and wrote on his work. Geoffrey Grigson, another important but entirely dissimilar critic, in a review reprinted in *Blessings, Kicks and Curses* (1982) also criticised Thomas's admirers, this time for alternately overindulging his few 'sentimental' poems or imagining him as representing 'the countryside party', to Grigson both equally damaging and misleading views. Something of Davie and Grigson's intelligent rejection of Thomas apologists can I think be seen in many essays in the present book, few of which show evidence of 'special pleading', and all of which take Thomas's work seriously enough and see it as important enough to both admire and quarrel with simultaneously. For instance, Robert Wells finds much wanting in Thomas's ideas of 'England'; Jeremy Hooker in a searching essay is able to find fault with much of the prose while also focusing on the best of it; Dick Davis concedes that much of Thomas's critical prose is "less than a pleasure to read" while clearly demonstrating how first rate much of it is too.

J.P. Ward's essay (reprinted from *Poetry Wales* and the only one not specially commissioned) advances the argument that Thomas has more in common with the Modernists than we might at first think. Several contributors mention Thomas as a poet involved in World War I, especially John Pikoulis, whose closely argued psychological and passionate approach is at variance with the tone of other essays. He alone in this anthology thinks that Thomas at one time considered divorce: I remain unconvinced by the meagre evidence for this view and dissociate myself from it while allowing John Pikoulis his opinion. John Bayley's characteristically precise look at the poems focuses on the words on the page and how specific poems — 'Adlestrop' included — work. A cultural and critical debate on separate aspects of Thomas's two countries of Wales and England is carried out in the contributions of Sally Roberts Jones and Robert Wells. Peter Levi supplies a valuable introductory essay on Thomas and his work.

These newly commissioned essays from both poets and critics make up a varied and diverse contemporary view of Edward Thomas as a prose writer, critic, anthologist; but mainly, of course, as poet. The book is planned to be of interest to the needs of different readers: from those approaching the work for the first time, to those interested in broad topics such as Modernism, the Folk Tradition, War Poetry etc., to a reader looking for the latest views on Thomas. The Chronology and Bibliography on page 11 presents both biographical and bibliographical information on books by Thomas and by critics on the work too for further reading.

Jonathan Barker, 1986

A Chronology of Edward Thomas's Life and Work: Incorporating a Bibliography of Books by and on Thomas

This chronology and bibliography is largely based on information contained in R. George Thomas's *Edward Thomas: A Portrait* (Oxford University Press 1985) and information from the same author collected elsewhere. I am indebted to R. George Thomas for permission to use his work as a source. All references to the poems use the numbering of R. George Thomas's edition of *The Collected Poems of Edward Thomas* (Oxford University Press, 1978) and appear thus: CP 4 'Old Man'; the dating of poems is as given by R. George Thomas.

Supplementary bibliographical information has been found in William Cooke's *Edward Thomas: A Critical Biography 1878-1917* (Faber, 1970). References to critical works on Edward Thomas include only books and not essays in periodicals. E.T. = Edward Thomas, R.G.T. = R. George Thomas, ed. = edited by, etc.

1878	3 March.	Philip Edward Thomas born, the eldest of six sons, at 10, Upper Lansdowne Road North, Lambeth, London, to Philip Henry Thomas (1854-1920) a native of Tredegar, and Mary Elizabeth Thomas (1853-1936) from Newport. Philip Henry was a staff clerk at the Board of Trade and a champion of Liberal politics, experienced public speaker, Nonconformist, Comtean Positivist, philanthropist, see CP 99 '[P.H.T.]'. Mary Elizabeth Thomas was a less austere, but nonetheless practical and pious woman. E.T.'s holidays spent with his grandmother in Swindon, Wiltshire or the Pontardulais region of Carmarthenshire, Wales; a life-long pattern.
1888		By this time the Thomas household had moved to 61, Shelgate Road, south London, E.T.'s home until Oxford.
1894		Having left Battersea Grammar School (where he met Arthur Hardy, a life-long friend) the previous year, E.T. attends St Paul's Public School. During his sixteenth year, encouraged by the journalist and critic James Ashcroft Noble, begins to write nature essays for publication in newspapers. By this time periodic depressions have begun. E.T. has developed life-long habit of long distance walks. Reading Richard Jefferies. Developing interest in natural history.
1895	March	Leaves St Paul's School intending to study at home for his first Civil Service examinations. Friendship develops between E.T. and the Wiltshire gamekeeper 'Dad' Uzzell.

	April	Frequent visitor to James Ashcroft Noble. Meets Helen Noble this year.
	Summer	Visit to Swindon. At this time keeps diary of 'field notes' later incorporated into *The Woodland Life*. Articles by E.T. published in *New Age*, the *Speaker*, the *Globe*.
1896	3 April	James Ashcroft Noble dies.
1897	May	E.T. working for Oxford entrance examinations.
	October	Passes Matriculation test. Now a non-collegiate student at Oxford preparing for entrance scholarships. Continues writing essays and some (unpublished) poems.
		At this time writing numerous letters to Helen Noble, and to Harry Hooton, a life-long friend and walking companion (E.T. dedicated *The Icknield Way* (1913) to Hooton) and eventually husband to Helen's friend Janet Aldis. *The Woodland Life* (Blackwood).
1898		At this time encouraged by his tutor Owen M. Edwards and his friend the Welsh bard and preacher Gwili (the Rev. John Jenkins). Wins history scholarship to Lincoln College, Oxford. Continues life-long friendship with Ian MacAlister from St Paul's and makes new friends, Fyffe, E.S.P. Haynes, J.H. Morgan, Wharton. Reading Walter Pater, Scott, Meredith, Hardy, Flaubert. Practises with dumb-bells, rows, continues long country walks. Continues writing essays. Takes laudanum for the first time.
1899	20 June	E.T. and Helen married at Fulham Registry Office without informing their parents. Janet Hooton and Mr Potbury witnesses.
	August	Harry Hooton informs both families of marriage. E.T. and Helen agree to use 61 Shelgate Road as a base. E.T. visits dying grandmother at Swindon, then to Pontardulais for three week holiday with his father's first cousin Philip Treharne Thomas. Then E.T. back at Oxford studying, drinking, swearing hard and in debt.
1900	15 January	Merfyn Thomas born.
	May	E.T. picks up mild gonococcal infection probably when drunkenly celebrating the Relief of Mafeking.
	June	Takes final examinations; awarded 2nd class honours. Pursues writing as a career.
	November	E.T. and Helen leave Shelgate Road and move to 117 Atheldane Road, Earlsfield, SW. E.T. freelance critic-essayist. Helen with a small and dwindling legacy.
1901	22 January	Queen Victoria dies; accession of King Edward VII.
		During this year E.T. and Helen move first to 7 Nightingale Parade, Nightingale Lane, Balham, SW. from where E.T. searches for work and reviews for the *Daily Chronicle* and the *World*; also articles in *Atlantic Monthly*, *Country Life*, *Outlook*, *Crampton's*. Later move to Rose Acre Cottage, Bearsted, Maidstone, Kent. E.T.

		suggesting projects to book publishers. Early this year E.T. meets Jesse Berridge, poet bank-clerk and eventually Anglican priest, who becomes a life-long friend. See *The Letters of Edward Thomas to Jesse Berridge* ed. Anthony Berridge (Enitharmon Press, 1983).
1902	31 May	Boer War ends.
	June	*Horae Solitariae* (Duckworth). First contact with their reader Edward Garnett, who becomes a life-long friend. Helen writes to a close friend, Janet Hooton "Even now poverty, anxiety, physical weakness, disappointments and discouragement are making him bitter, hard, and impatient, quick to violent anger, and subject to long fits of depression...".
	30 September	E.T. writes first letter to Gordon Bottomley, poet and dramatist, to become a life-long friend. See *Letters from Edward Thomas to Gordon Bottomley* ed. R. George Thomas (Oxford University Press, 1968).
	29 October	Birth of Bronwen Thomas.
	December	Following death of Lionel Johnson in October E.T. takes over as regular reviewer for the *Daily Chronicle*.
1903	February	H.W. Nevinson obtains commission for E.T. to write *Oxford* by 30th June. E.T. working away from home.
	June	Move of E.T. and family to The Green, Bearsted, Kent.
	October	E.T. in depressed and nervous state. Consults Dr Segundo. Continues experiment of working away from home for short periods. *The Poems of John Dyer* ed. E.T. (Fisher Unwin), *Oxford* paintings by John Fulleylove (Black).
1904	January	Meets Arthur Ransome.
	May	Move to Elses Farm, The Weald, near Sevenoaks, Kent.
	Summer	MacAlister visits E.T. on return from Canada. Other visitors include Jesse Berridge, Arthur Ransome, Harry Hooton.
	September	E.T. takes rooms in Ransome's lodgings, 1 Gunter Grove, Chelsea for one month to write. *Rose Acre Papers* (Brown Langham).
1905	October	Writes "short ejaculations in prose". Meets W.H. Hudson, Walter De La Mare and W.H. Davies, the latter at the Farmhouse hostel, Marshalsea Road, Southwark, following E.T.'s favourable review of *The Soul's Destroyer*. E.T. invites W.H. Davies to share his study at Stidulph's Cottage, Egg Pie Lane, The Weald, Kent. E.T. reviewing for the *Daily Chronicle*, the *Speaker*, the *World*, the *Academy*. Regular visits to St George's Restaurant, St Martin's Lane: *habitués* include Walter De La Mare, Ralph Hodgson and later W.H. Davies. C.F. Cazenove now E.T.'s literary agent.
		Beautiful Wales (Black). E.T. contributes a poem,

		'Eluned', as a pseudo-translation.
1906		E.T. regularly reviewing books and visiting the British Museum in Bloomsbury, and Fleet Street editors and publishers. Visits the Mont Blanc, Gerrard Street, Soho: *habitués* include Thomas Seccombe, R.A. Scott-James, Stephen Reynolds, W.H. Davies, Hilaire Belloc, Ford Madox Hueffer, et al.
	February	W.H. Davies moves into Stidulph's Cottage, Egg Pie Lane and works on *The Autobiography of a Super-Tramp.* Various regular weekend visitors to Elses Farm.
	March	E.T. visits Gordon Bottomley at Cartmel, Westmorland. During this year the lease expires on Elses Farm and by December the family move to Berryfield Cottage, Ashford Chase Estate, near Petersfield, Hants., close to Bedales School which Merfyn attends.
		The Heart of England (Dent), *The Bible in Spain* by George Borrow, ed. E.T. (Dent).
1907		Helen teaching at Bedales preparatory school, and eventually also taking in boarders. E.T. on frequent visits to London, reviewing and working on his biography of Richard Jefferies. Visits specialist in neurasthenia. *The Pocket Book of Poems and Songs for the Open Air* comp. E.T. (E. Grant Richards), *British Country Life in Spring and Summer* (Hodder & Stoughton).
1908		At about this time E.T. infatuated with a teenage girl, Hope Webb, (one time charge of Helen) when writing *Richard Jefferies* at Minsmere, Suffolk. Geoffrey Lupton offers to build a new family house at Wick Green, Steep, Hants. E.T. for a time Assistant Secretary to Royal Commission on Ancient Monuments and living in London, working in the British Museum Library in the evenings. *British Country Life in Autumn and Winter* (Hodder & Stoughton), *The Temple and A Priest to the Temple* by George Herbert, ed. E.T. (Dent), *Some British Birds* (Hodder & Stoughton), *British Butterflies and Other Insects* (Hodder & Stoughton).
1909		E.T. working in new study, The Bee-house; by end of year family move to new William Morris house, Wick Green, Steep, Hants. E.T. gives up Dr Savitt. *Richard Jefferies: His Life and Work* (Hutchinson), *The Plays and Poems of Christopher Marlowe* ed. E.T. (Dent), *The Hills and the Vales* by Richard Jefferies ed. E.T. (Duckworth), *The South Country* (Dent), *Ezra Pound Personae* (Elkin Mathews).
1910	6 May	Accession of King George V on death of Edward VII.
	16 August	Myfanwy Thomas born.
		Windsor Castle (Blackie), *Rose Acre Papers* (Duckworth), *Feminine Influence on the Poets* (Secker), *Rest and Unrest* (Duckworth).

1911 E.T. with Edward Garnett arranges civil list pension for W.H. Davies. E.T. in poor health despite attempt to give up smoking and new vegetarian diet. Continues to write sketches and tales. At work on many projects simultaneously and under great strain. At end of year moves into boarding house, Laugharne, Carmarthenshire to write. *Light and Twilight* (Duckworth), *Words and Places in Illustration of History...* by Isaac Taylor, ed. E.T. (Dent), *Maurice Maeterlinck* (Methuen), *The Tenth Muse* (Secker), *Celtic Stories* (Oxford University Press), *The Isle of Wight* (Blackie).

1912 E.T. writing for *New Age*, *English Review*, *Poetry and Drama*. On visit to Clifford Bax at Broughton Gifford, Wiltshire receives treatment for his "disordered intellect" diagnosed as 'neurasthenia' (Gordon Bottomley also claimed E.T. had an undiagnosed "diabetic tendency" which "tormented him"). Writing books on Pater and Swinburne.

November — Leaves Wick Green to stay with Vivian Locke Ellis at Selsfield House, East Grinstead where he writes *The Happy-Go-Lucky Morgans*. Short trip to Paris. Meets Eleanor Farjeon.

December — *Georgian Poetry 1911-1912* (Poetry Bookshop), edited by Edward Marsh (although his name does not appear on the title page). The first of the five influential and popular anthologies published between 1912-1922. Sales of this volume alone eventually totalled 15,000 copies making the contributors a fair sum from royalties. *Lafcadio Hearn* (Constable), *Norse Tales* (Oxford University Press), *Rural Rides* by William Cobbett, ed. E.T. (Dent), *The Pocket George Borrow* selected by E.T. (Chatto & Windus), *Algernon Charles Swinburne: A Critical Study* (Secker), *George Borrow the Man and His Books* (Chapman & Hall).

1913 E.T. still reviewing for Harold Monro's *Poetry and Drama*, also *Daily Chronicle* and other journals. Serves on *Poetry Review* panel who award prize to Rupert Brooke's 'Grantchester' although E.T. votes for Ralph Hodgson. E.T.'s health deteriorates. Visits Clifford Bax at Broughton Gifford.

July — Move to Yew Tree Cottage in Steep Village, Petersfield, Hants.

August — Introduces Eleanor Farjeon to the family; Eleanor becomes friend and support to Helen and secretary to E.T..

October — E.T. away from Steep until early February 1914 at East Grinstead and in London writing. Introduced by Ralph Hodgson to Robert Frost. Frost had already published *A Boy's Will* and written most of the poems for *North of Boston*

		and *Mountain Interval*.
	December	E.T. meets Frost again at St George's Restaurant, St Martin's Lane. This intense empathising, short-lived friendship was to be a stimulus to both men. See E.T. CP 119 'The sun used to shine' and Frost's 'To E.T.' *New Hampshire* (1923) and 'Iris by Night' *A Further Range* (1936). *The Happy-Go-Lucky Morgans* (Duckworth), W.H. Hudson wrote to Edward Garnett of this book "He is essentially a poet...and this book shows it, I think, more than any of the others". E.T. working on *The Childhood of Edward Thomas* at Selsfield House. *The Country* (Batsford), *The Icknield Way* (Constable), *Walter Pater: A Critical Study* (Secker).
1914	January	E.T. still away from home.
	February	E.T. awarded £100 by Royal Literary Fund; application supported by Hudson, Garnett, De La Mare, Davies, Belloc. Return to Steep, which from now remains his permanent home until family move to High Beech in 1916.
	April	E.T. away with Merfyn and Bronwen in Wales and with Robert Frost in Herefordshire. *In Pursuit of Spring* (Nelson).
	July	E.T. reviews Robert Frost's *North of Boston* in *Daily News*.
	4 August	Great Britain declares war against Germany. E.T. visit this month to Frosts at Ledington, near Ledbury, Hereford. (In October 1917 Frost was to write to Amy Lowell re E.T. "1914 was our year. I never had, I never shall have another such year of friendship".) Nearby Frost were the Chandler family, and a group of writers including W.W. Gibson, Lascelles Abercrombie and their wives and later Eleanor Farjeon. See W.W. Gibson's 'The Golden Room' *The Golden Room* (Macmillan, 1928) for a portrait of the community.
	September	E.T. considering leaving for U.S.A. with Frost.
	October	E.T. cycling tour in Wales. First prose drafts of poems in notebooks. Steep.
	December	First drafts of poems "begin to run". Writes CP 1-15. Sends poems to Frost. Steep.
	3 December	CP 1 'Up in the Wind'. Steep.
	6 December	CP 4 'Old Man' (R.G.T. notes similarities with the opening of *The Childhood of Edward Thomas* and an unpublished story 'The Old House' of 1909). Steep.
	8-13 December	CP 6 'The Other' (R.G.T. notes this poem is indebted to parts of *In Pursuit of Spring* (1914), the book Robert Frost told E.T. proved he was more poet than prose writer). Steep. Mid-December. CP 10 'The Mountain Chapel' (R.G.T. notes that this poem uses memories of visits to Wales). Steep. *The Zincali: An Account of the Gipsies of Spain*

		by George Borrow, ed. E.T. (Dent).
1915	January	E.T. confined to Yew Tree Cottage with severely sprained ankle. This month writes CP 16-32. Steep.
	8 January	CP 21 'Adlestrop' (R.G.T. note shows preceded by a prose passage).
	February	This month writes poems CP 33-39. E.T. sending poems to friends and editors under the pseudonym of Edward Eastaway.
	11 February	CP 34 'Parting' (R.G.T. notes this poem recalls the departure of Merfyn for America with the Frosts). Steep.
	March	This month writes CP 40-53. Steep.
	April	Harold Monro turns down book of poems by E.T. for publication. This month writes CP 54-68. Mostly at Steep.
	3-4 April	CP 56 'Lob' E.T.'s most sustained homage to the folklore and folk traditions.
	May	Writing *The Life of the Duke of Marlborough*. This month writes CP 69-75 and thereby completes over half his output of poems in six months. Steep.
	June	Finishes Marlborough life. E.T. still considering joining the Frosts in America. This month writes CP 76-77. Hucclecote.
	July	Enlists in the Artists' Rifles. Writes CP 78-88. Steep and London.
	August	Billeted with his parents in London.
	21 September	Robert Frost writes to Lascelles Abercrombie that the war "has made some sort of new man and a poet out of Edward Thomas".
	October	Camp at High Beech, Epping, Essex and London H.Q. Visits friends at St George's Restaurant and Lyons near Burton Road and Tottenham Court Road. CP 89 'October'.
	November	E.T. made Lance Corporal map reading instructor training young officers, Hare Hall Camp, near Romford, Essex. Writes CP 90-92.
	26 November	CP 92 'Liberty'.
	26 December	CP 93 'This is no case of petty right or wrong'. Steep. Merfyn returns from America. *Four-and-Twenty Blackbirds* (Duckworth), *This England: An Anthology from her Writers* comp. E.T. (Oxford University Press), includes 'Haymaking' and 'The Manor Farm' by Edward Eastaway, *The Life of the Duke of Marlborough* (Chapman & Hall).
1916	January	E.T. transferred to a new Company at Hare Hall Camp. Writes CP 94-96.
	7 January	CP 94 'Rain' (R.G.T. notes similarities to a prose passage from *The Icknield Way* pp.280-3 (1913)).
	February	London and Steep on convalescent leave. Writes CP 97-

	102.
8 February	CP 99 '[P.H.T.]' addressed to E.T.'s father.
11 February	CP 101 '[M.E.T.]'. (R.G.T. notes that this poem is addressed to E.T.'s mother and titles accordingly; most commentators, however, conclude this poem is probably addressed to Helen).
March	Promoted to full Corporal. Still considering going to America after the war. Sends batch of poems to Gordon Bottomley from which eighteen are selected for inclusion, under the name Edward Eastaway in an *An Annual of New Poetry* (1917). Writes CP 103-105. *Keats* (Jack). This spring sees publication of Robert Graves's first book *Over the Brazier* (Poetry Bookshop).
29 March-9 April	Writes CP 106-109, 'Household Poems' for Bronwen, Merfyn, Myfanwy, Helen. Little Warley and Hare Hall Camp.
22-30 April	Writes CP 110-111.
May	Completes CP 112-121. Hare Hall Camp.
5 May	CP 115 'I never saw that land before'.
22 May	CP 119 'The sun used to shine', E.T.'s poem to Robert Frost.
27 May	CP 121 'As the team's head brass'.
June	Writes CP 122-128. Hare Hall Camp. Awarded a grant of £300 by the Government instead of a Civil List Pension. Applies for a Commission in the Royal Artillery, with the possibility of active service. E.T. and Helen on walking tour visiting Guthries, Hootons, Ellises and Eleanor Farjeon. At this time E.T. instructing the artists Paul Nash and John Wheatley in map reading.
July	Writes CP 129-132. Selsfield, Steep, Hare Hall Camp.
August	Leaves Hare Hall Camp, posted to Royal Artillery School, Handel Street, London WC. Billeted with parents in Balham. Submits poems to the publisher Roger Ingpen. Writes CP 133 'The Swifts'.
September	Unit moved to Trowbridge, Wiltshire towards the end of the month. Writes CP 134-137.
October	Family move from Steep to 2 Paul's Nursery, High Beech, Epping, Essex. Writes CP 138 ['The Child in the Orchard']. *The Flowers I Love* comp. E.T., drawings Katherine Cameron (Jack).
November	Volunteers for overseas duty. Latter part of the month spent on final leave. Writes CP 139-141. CP 139 'Lights Out'. Trowbridge. CP 140 'The long small room'. Trowbridge. (Possibly based on his study bedroom at 61 Shelgate Road.) *Six Poems* by Edward Eastaway (Pear Tree Press).
December	Commissioned 2nd Lieutenant. Posted to Officers' Mess, Tin Town, Lydd, Kent for final training. Writes CP 142-

		143.
	24 December	CP 143 'Out in the Dark'. High Beech.
1917	January	Begins Diary (which runs until 8 April, the day before E.T.'s death). At Lydd, then mobilisation leave with parents in Balham, Helen in High Beech, London to see friends, and farewells to family at High Beech. Firing practice at Codford, near Warminster, Wiltshire.
	13 January	Writes CP 144 'Last Poem "The sorrow of true love" ', Lydd, (R.G.T. notes that this poem appears on the final page of the Diary kept by E.T. and probably on his body when he died).
	29 January	Embarkation from Southampton to Le Havre.
	February	Battery positioned near Arras. E.T. to Group H.Q. inspecting batteries. CP 4 'Old Man', CP 78 'The Word', CP 102 'The Unknown' published in *Poetry* (Chicago) Vol.IX by Edward Eastaway.
	March	E.T. at front line trenches, Observation Posts Ronville and Beaurains; then routine duties at Battery H.Q., practising, supervising dug-outs and shallow trenches, shelling enemy positions. *An Annual of New Poetry* (Constable) with eighteen poems by Edward Eastaway.
	April	Under fire. Preparation for Arras offensive.
	9 April	E.T. killed 7.36 a.m. by blast from a stray shell at Beaurains Observation Post.
	14 April	E.T.'s death reported in the *Times*.
	June	T.S. Eliot *Prufrock and Other Observations* (Egoist).
	October	*Poems* by Edward Thomas (Edward Eastaway) (Selwyn & Blount). *A Literary Pilgrim in England* (Methuen).
1918		*Last Poems* by Edward Thomas (Selwyn & Blount).
	October	W.H. Davies *Forty New Poems* (Fifield) includes 'Killed in Action (Edward Thomas)'. Davies described E.T. as "my first and oldest literary friend".
	11 November	Armistice signed by Germany.
1920		*Collected Poems* Edward Thomas with foreword by Walter De La Mare (Selwyn & Blount).
1922	February	*Ulysses* by James Joyce (Shakespeare & Co.).
	October	'The Waste Land' by T.S. Eliot in the *Criterion* Vol.I No.1.
	November	*Georgian Poetry 1920-1922* (Poetry Bookshop). The last in the series, not one of which contained a poem by E.T..
		Cloud Castle and Other Papers by Edward Thomas with a foreword by W.H. Hudson (Duckworth).
1926		*Essays of To-day and Yesterday* (Harrap), *Chosen Essays* (Gregynog Press), Helen Thomas *As It Was* (Heinemann), Edward Thomas *The Augustan Books of Poetry* (Benn).
1927		Edward Thomas *Selected Poems* ed. Edward Garnett (Gregynog Press), Edward Thomas *Two Poems* (Ingpen & Grant).

1928		Edward Thomas *The Last Sheaf: Essays* Foreword by Thomas Seccombe (Cape), Edward Thomas *Collected Poems* (Ingpen & Grant) rev. ed. with four more poems.
1931		Helen Thomas *World Without End* (Heinemann).
1932		F.R. Leavis *New Bearings in English Poetry* (Chatto).
1935		Helen Thomas *As It Was and World Without End* (Heinemann), *These Things the Poets' Said* Foreword by R.P. Eckert (Pear Tree Press).
1936		Edward Thomas *Collected Poems* (Faber & Faber).
1937	October	The Edward Thomas Memorial Committee place the Sarsen Stone Memorial on the shoulder of Mutton Hanger above Steep.
		R.P. Eckert *Edward Thomas: A Biography and a Bibliography* (Dent).
1938		Edward Thomas *The Childhood of Edward Thomas* Preface by Julian Thomas (Faber & Faber), Edward Thomas *The Friend of the Blackbird* (Pear Tree Press).
1939		John Moore *The Life and Letters of Edward Thomas* (Heinemann).
1940	26 September	Death of W.H. Davies.
		Edward Thomas *The Trumpet and Other Poems* (Faber & Faber).
1948		Death of Gordon Bottomley.
		Edward Thomas *The Prose of Edward Thomas* ed. Roland Gant (Falcon Press).
1949		Edward Thomas *Collected Poems* (Faber & Faber) 5th impression with additional poem CP 99 '[P.H.T.]'. 141 poems.
1951		Clifford Bax *Some I Knew Well* (Phoenix House).
1955		*Poet and Painter: Being the Correspondence Between Gordon Bottomley and Paul Nash* ed. Claude Colleer Abbott & Anthony Bertram (Oxford University Press).
1956		H. Coombes *Edward Thomas: A Critical Study* (Chatto & Windus).
		Death of Walter De La Mare.
1958		Eleanor Farjeon *Edward Thomas: The Last Four Years* (Oxford University Press).
1959		Christopher Hassall *Edward Marsh: Patron of the Arts* (Faber & Faber).
1960		Edward Thomas *Pocket Poets Series* (Vista Books).
1962		Vernon Scannell *Edward Thomas* in British Council Writers and Their Work Series (Longmans, Green), Edward Thomas *Selected Poems* ed. Robin Skelton (Hutchinson), *Georgian Poetry* ed. James Reeves (Penguin).
1963	29 January	Death of Robert Frost.
		Richard J. Stonesifer *W.H. Davies: A Critical Biography* (Cape).

1964		Edward Thomas *Selected Poems* ed. R.S. Thomas (Faber & Faber), *Up the Line to Death* ed. Brian Gardner (Methuen).
1965	2 August	Death of Merfyn Thomas.
		Edward Thomas *The Green Roads* ed. Eleanor Farjeon (Bodley Head), Robert Frost *Selected Letters* ed. Lawrance Thompson (Cape), Bernard Bergonzi *Heroes' Twilight* (Constable), *Men Who March Away* ed. I.M. Parsons (Chatto & Windus).
1967	12 April	Death of Helen Thomas.
		Joy Grant *Harold Monro and the Poetry Bookshop* (Routledge & Kegan Paul), Robert H. Ross *The Georgian Revolt: Rise and Fall of a Poetic Ideal 1910-22* (Faber & Faber).
1968		*Letters from Edward Thomas to Gordon Bottomley* ed. R. George Thomas (Oxford University Press).
1970		William Cooke *Edward Thomas: A Critical Biography 1878-1917* (Faber & Faber).
1971		*The Poetry of Robert Frost* ed. Edward Connery Lathem (Cape)
1972		*Edward Thomas* by R. George Thomas (University of Wales Press).
1973		Edward Thomas *Poems and Last Poems* ed. Edna Longley (Collins).
1975	29 March	Death of Bronwen Thomas.
1977		*Georgian Poetry 1911-1922: the Critical Heritage* ed. Timothy Rogers (Routledge & Kegan Paul), *Edward Thomas on the Countryside* ed. Roland Gant (Faber & Faber).
1978		Edward Thomas *The Collected Poems of Edward Thomas* ed. and intro. by R. George Thomas (Oxford University Press), the standard text; Jan Marsh *Edward Thomas: A Poet for his Country* (Elek), *Poetry Wales* Edward Thomas Centenary Issue Vol. 13 No.4 Spring ed. J.P. Ward, Helen Thomas *Time and Again* ed. Myfanwy Thomas (Carcanet Press), Edward Thomas *Reading Out of Doors* (Tragara Press), Edward Thomas *Four Letters of Frederick Evans* (Privately printed), William Cooke *Edward Thomas: A Portrait* (Hub Publications).
1980		Andrew Motion *The Poetry of Edward Thomas* (Routledge & Kegan Paul).
1981		Edward Thomas *The Collected Poems of Edward Thomas* ed. and intro. by R. George Thomas (Oxford University Press) shortened paperback edition, *The Chessplayer and Other Essays* intro. R. George Thomas (Whittington Press), *A language not to be betrayed: Selected Prose of Edward Thomas* ed. Edna Longley (Carcanet Press), Edward Thomas *Selected Poems and Prose* ed. David Wright (Penguin), Edward Thomas *A Selection of Letters to Edward Garnett* (Tragara Press).
1982		Myfanwy Thomas *One of These Fine Days* (Carcanet

		Press), Edward Thomas *The Fear of Death: A Story* (Tragara Press), Ivor Gurney *Collected Poems* ed. P.J. Kavanagh (Oxford University Press).
1983		Edward Thomas *A Sportsman's Tale* intro. R. George Thomas (Tragara Press), *The Letters of Edward Thomas to Jesse Berridge*, with a memoir by Jesse Berridge ed. and intro. Anthony Berridge (Enitharmon Press).
1985	11 November	Memorial to sixteen World War I poets (including E.T.) unveiled in Westminster Abbey Poets' Corner by Ted Hughes, Poet Laureate.
		R. George Thomas *Edward Thomas: A Portrait* (Oxford University Press)
1986		Michael Kirkham *The Imagination of Edward Thomas* (Cambridge University Press), Stan Smith *Edward Thomas* (Faber & Faber), Edna Longley *Poetry in the Wars* (Bloodaxe Books) includes two essays on Edward Thomas.

PETER LEVI

Notes on Edward Thomas

Notes on Edward Thomas

I doubt whether it serves much purpose to call Edward Thomas a great, a major or a minor poet; he was certainly genuine, authentic, a true poet, and that is rare enough to be important. He has for us a further importance, because of his precise, late Victorian generation which stood in 1914 on the threshold of a new poetry. *Georgian Poetry* was not quite a movement, but a series of anthologies published between 1912 and 1922, which included highly untypical contributors; Georgianism is not a proper blanket term for an entire generation. And yet many poets at that time faced up to the same problems in their different ways, because the problems were in the language, though it was Edward Thomas of all of them who found the most interesting solutions. Analogies exist in the musical culture of England in the same period. It is only now that I can understand why I preferred him to the other so-called war poets and the so-called Georgian poets, when I was nineteen or earlier. I had also read his prose, which in those days was still lying about, and admired it greatly.

He was brought up in an atmosphere of not abnormal Victorian middle-class high-mindedness and strained aesthetic feelings; his moral background was as debilitating as Browning's, and Tennyson has no entry in the index of his latest biography, because Tennyson was out of fashion, and English poetry was busily and ccomplacently getting lost. He took extreme views about style and stylishness partly from Flaubert, and to some extent from Pater, and many years passed before he could break through that crust. He took over his book reviewing job on the *Chronicle* from Lionel Johnson. He was keen on the rhythms of vernacular speech, just as Robert Frost was, and Pound was, but he scarcely broke free of archaisms and sublime sentiments except in a handful of poems. It is hard to think one's way back into his world. His true contemporaries were W.H. Davies and Hilaire Belloc and Walter De La Mare. He greatly enjoyed a parody of Masefield, and as a literary judge wanted to give Ralph Hodgson the prize that in fact went to Rupert Brooke's 'Grantchester'.

He had a William Morris cottage built for him in 1908 convenient for the progressive school at Bedales where his children were pupils and his wife taught. It took him until nearly forty to clear his head of such overgrown shrubbery worthies as Lewis Morris and Maeterlinck and Jefferies. His familiar intimacy with the English countryside was sodden through and through with high-minded feelings. If one reads Jefferies and then the prose of Edward Thomas and the poem 'Lob' he was so proud of, and then lastly the Brensham novels of his biographer John Moore, one observes that the waters disturbed by the Victorians took more than a hundred years to clear. It is therefore not as easy as it looks to place Edward Thomas in any way or to trace his development. He felt free of religion and yet he was still heavily burdened with soul. He surely had friends who wore home-woven knickerbockers. The habit of laudanum and the depressing experience of undiagnosed diabetes cannot have helped. His attitudes to his marriage did not make for and did not achieve success, but he depended very deeply on his wife, and her prose masterpieces, *As it Was* (1926) and *World Without End* (1931), are perhaps his best monument, and certainly still the best avenue of approach to the thoughts and feelings of that distant time. We are nearly as distant now from the floruit of Edward Thomas as he was from the floruit of Keats and Shelley, his ideal poets.

Even within his own generation, his standing is not easily defined. He had never read Laforgue or Eliot, and French poetry had no discernible influence on him. He thought Imagism was silly, though R. George Thomas points out that he did give a good review to Pound's *Personae* in the *Daily Chronicle* (1909). But one must remember that his criticism was written before his poetry, and most of his recorded remarks and enthusiasms, even those he shared with Frost, predate his own practice as a poet. Ballads and traditional poems nourished his imagination for years; he and Belloc used to sing together, and he sang his own songs in the army, but his personal poetry took another tone. To put the problem at its baldest, his inwardness with nature was no more impressive than Flora Thompson's and less so than John Clare's or Geoffrey Grigson's; he had something to say but less than Hardy had, he was wonderfully self-expressive of grief and loneliness, but not more memorably than Walter De La Mare, and not more individually than Ivor Gurney. Yet I think the word individuality is the clue to our very high estimate of him.

Robert Wells put the point I want to make in his review of the biography by R. George Thomas (*T.L.S.* October 4th, 1985). I have been leading up to this.

> This biography reveals how, almost from the beginning of his career, Thomas struggled to shed the mannerism which, he complained, came naturally to him, and to arrive at "living and social words". The need, he came to realise, was to find a poetic technique for reflecting the idiosyncrasies of the individual voice, in the absence of any shared belief. He wanted "an increasing fineness, an increasing subtlety of aim, a deepening of the palimpsest...so that more and more the writing reflects not merely the main features of a man's character." He maintained a metrical structure in his verse; his innovation lay in the extent to which he allowed a

> personal speech rhythm to interrupt it. The poetry of 'personality' which he foresaw now provides the convention in which we swim.

This is surely true, and it explains why we listen to Edward Thomas with such a very close personal attention, while the eloquent rhetoric of other poets of his age passes us by, and those extreme statements that seem so convincing at first drop away from us in the end, while his insidiously personal voice remains. It also explains why the purely metrical power of Belloc and his Parnassian crispness and clarity have ceased to attract imitations. They lack intimacy. There is no doubt that the personal voice of Edward Thomas, including its tragic undertones, affects his poetry as a sound, not just as a medium of expression. Subtlety of expression is impossible without technique, but it adds a new sound, a new range of tones, to technique, in poetry as in music. Rimbaud's youthful success as a poet was in part surely because he had too much to say. The late maturing attainment of Edward Thomas was because he had so much not to say but to express. There is a sense, which he himself recognised, in which Edward Thomas never knew himself until he wrote his poetry.

The long poem 'Lob', which is about the eternal character of the English countryman, is not exactly a self-expression, but a condensation of old themes dear to the poet's heart, something he had to get off his chest. I think he needed to do that in order to move forward. The later chance woodland meetings in his verses are much more ominous. He is sometimes as close to Kafka as he is to Hardy, or to his own everyday prose accounts of the same scenes. The places in his poetry are often composite. No one knows quite where 'The long small room' is set, though candidates do exist. The poem is deeply expressive of Edward Thomas, perhaps for the very reason that it arises in part at least from his interest in Japanese verse technique. "As a matter of fact I started with the last line as what I was working to. I am only fearing it has a sort of Japanesy suddenness of ending." His letter makes it clear that the vivid effects of this last line had been too powerful for the taste of Eleanor Farjeon (c.f. *Collected Poems*, ed. R. George Thomas, note to poem 140). Maybe she feared its meaning. I do not think there is any doubt that Chinese and Japanese poetry were a principal source of that peculiar interfusion of personal feeling and objective nature aesthetically perceived which Thomas pioneered in English, though we now know them better through Ezra Pound and Arthur Waley, who came later and more directly to this subject, and through the Penguin Classics. It is essential to the personal tone of Edward Thomas as it was to the plays of Chekhov and of Pirandello, that much more is implied than is said. He rightly remarked that only one who put his whole self into his verses had the right or ability to detain another person's attention.

In this poem there is a slight awkwardness of phrasing, a prosaic exactness, which in the end strengthens the effect of each four line stanza. Even the scansion seems to stutter before it takes hold:

> The long small room that showed the willows in the west
> Narrowed up to the end the fireplace filled,
> Although not wide. I liked it. No one guessed
> What need or accident made them so build.

Each of the first three stanzas has what might seem to be too many syllables in the first line. To say that if they are spoken they are perfect, or that they convey a conversational tone, is not enough. The rhythmic unit is the stanza, and then the whole poem. One hears it as one hears a musical phrase in context, it comes to rest as it finishes but not before. The first stanza is by far the most awkward, and deliberately so. I am not quite certain that the full stop after "wide" is right, but I think it is, and let us assume so. In the second stanza the rhythm is smoother, though once again a full stop ends it.

> Only the moon, the mouse and the sparrow peeped
> In from the ivy round the casement thick.
> Of all they saw and heard there they shall keep
> The tale for the old ivy and older brick.

In the first stanza the room is only strange, though one assumes that the willows in the west are beautiful. We are in an old house among water-meadows. In the next stanza the room and the house are eerie, but still no human being is present. It is night. We are falling in love with this ancient and empty place. The third stanza flows straight into the fourth, and the rhythm slides like water. In three lines we have utterly deserted the message of mere rustic or romantic melancholy beauty that the second stanza began to suggest. By the way in which he enters the poem Edward Thomas has transformed its opening into a brilliant and painful metaphor for his own life. The absence and the sadness are his, and the final stanza is strong autobiography. The last line is shattering and unforgettable. It completes the process of giving meaning and force to what had seemed to be a quiet meditative exercise. We know of course that it was written first.

> When I look back I am like moon, sparrow and mouse
> That witnessed what they could never understand
> Or alter or prevent in the dark house.
> One thing remains the same — this my right hand
>
> Crawling crab-like over the clean white page,
> Resting awhile each morning on the pillow,
> Then once more starting to crawl on towards age.
> The hundred last leaves stream upon the willow.

We had to wait for Larkin for any more poems like that. None of the other poets killed in the war had written anything so powerful when they died, except for the pathos of death or of their own deaths. Edward Thomas was writing about his whole life and self. The absence of the observing moon becomes dreadful when it is his own absence from his life and its consequences, and the movement of his hand becomes terrible and impersonal, a movement towards death. The poem seems to me perfect. It hardly needs even this amount of simplistic exegesis; the reader who pays attention to its details will find them telling. By being impersonal the poem becomes most deeply personal. The interweaving of sentence endings and stanza endings, and the degree of syntactic variation towards a climax recall the practice of Horace in his meditative lyrics.

This was a new style in English poetry. I have the sensation that Meredith was an important influence on Edward Thomas, but not a precise influence, so that we shall probably never understand quite how that worked until a new poet is found who loves Meredith in the same way as he did. However that may be, there is no doubting his originality. It now seems to be widely accepted that it was not the war which made him a poet at last when he was nearly forty. The momentum of his life was towards it, and the courageous leap was overdue. He always had the literary stubbornness, the need to work things out for himself, and the dogged persistence of a poet. The problem is that two transformations quite different in themselves took place in him at the same time. Firstly, he became a poet, and secondly, once his mind was made up, he stopped mooning and transformed himself into a most efficient soldier. Nothing could have seemed so unlikely for a mild and wandering literary man in early middle age, given to rustic meditations and on the edge of becoming a professional lecturer. I do not think the one change has much to do with the other, unless by removing the need and the possibility of endless aesthetic prose, the army may have set him free to be the poet he most purely was. But the same thing could have happened otherwise. His death was a tragic accident; he had certainly not reached the end of his development, or by any means the limits of his talent.

The poems of his I liked most as a boy were mostly not free of his old Shelleyan romanticism. At the same period I tried to think well of Maurice Baring as a poet, and I was innocent of the modern movement. I liked his invocation to 'Words', which I classed with a similar poem by James Elroy Flecker, and 'The Trumpet' and 'Lights Out' for their subject matter. 'The Trumpet' splendidly expresses its boyish sentiments, and it has beautiful lines and a splendid cumulative rhythm. It will not do, of course. "Up with the light,/ To the old wars" gives it away, and it could hardly have been written after 1918, though I am glad that it once was, because it comforted me. I think Edward Thomas was instructor in map-reading in the Artists' Rifles to two of my uncles, both of whom were killed in their first fortnight in the trenches as young officers, almost schoolboys; I expect they would have liked 'The Trumpet'. "I have written some verses suggested by the trumpet calls which go all day...the Reveille pleases me." (c.f. *Collected Poems* ed. R. George Thomas, note to poem 137).

'Lights Out' is a more serious proposition. It returns to his old metaphor of the woods and reminds me of another old romantic favourite of my boyhood, Belloc's translation of a line from the *Chanson de Roland*, "Hauts sont li puys at ténébreux et grants", as "High are the hills and dark and full of sleep". It is worth pointing out that the sentiment is real, to the experience of night walking, and in experience frightening. The long country wanderings of Edward Thomas and of Belloc took place when the railways carried everything and everyone, there were almost no cars, and the roads were unmade and most of them nearly deserted. Silence and even darkness itself have now nearly ceased to exist. No forest in Britain is unfathomable. 'The Trumpet' looks different to us because our mood has altered. In the case of 'Lights Out', nothing has altered but the countryside, and the imminence of death to soldiers in 1916. He wrote it in November of that year, about a week before 'The long small room'. Only four more poems were to come. He went to France at the end of January 1917 and died in April. The last fragmentary line that he scribbled in his war diary was "Roads shining like river up hill after rain."

I have come to the borders of sleep,
The unfathomable deep
Forest, where all must lose
Their way, however straight
Or winding, soon or late;
They can not choose.

Many a road and track
That since the dawn's first crack
Up to the forest brink
Deceived the travellers,
Suddenly now blurs,
And in they sink.

Here love ends –
Despair, ambition ends;
All pleasure and all trouble,
Although most sweet or bitter,
Here ends, in sleep that is sweeter
Than tasks most noble.

There is not any book
Or face of dearest look
That I would not turn from now
To go into the unknown

I must enter, and leave, alone,
I know not how.

The tall forest towers:
Its cloudy foliage lowers
Ahead, shelf above shelf:
Its silence I hear and obey
That I may lose my way
And myself.

This poem, 'Lights Out', aspires to the condition of music, it is from one point of view little more than a musical exercise. "It sums up what I have often thought at that call. I wish it were as brief— 2 pairs of long notes." (c.f. *Collected Poems* ed. R. George Thomas, note to poem 139). He had his doubts about this poem, and it was unrevised at his death. But has it not a power of its own? And can that power be dissociated from its long musical breathing? It seems too long, and yet it works cumulatively. It modulates from verse to verse and mood to mood towards its final truthfulness, which was otherwise perhaps unattainable. It is all metaphor, and all real. Its apparently comforting pieces of Georgian impedimenta, such as the tasks most noble, and the "face of dearest look", have in their context and by contrast a chilling effect, an emptiness. The rhythms of the stanzas vary from one another, and they become more gripping. After the marvellous first line, the self is forgotten, or swallowed up in metaphor, until its forceful re-entry in the third line of the fourth stanza. The last stanza is the truth about himself, and I suppose it is the most chilling of all. And the forest seen from close is a powerful presence. I do not think it matters that to some readers it will recall Keats. It is real enough for its deadly purpose. One might say its suicidal purpose.

Edward Thomas is a particular master of opening lines, and this is always because of their personal cadences: 'October' for instance:

The green elm with the one great bough of gold
Lets leaves into the grass slip, one by one.

The language is undoubtedly literary, so is even the colouring (gold is a more useful rhyming word than yellow), and the word order is gratuitously odd. W.H. Auden would have covered these lines in red pencil marks. Yet listen to the two lines. They could be by no-one else, and they have a wonderful movement of sounds. The rhyme-scheme of this poem is extremely subtle and indirect, and thereby the more effective. Its first version, which I have never seen, was apparently in blank verse. The very light, almost irregular, scarcely heard chimes it has now suggest that Edward Thomas had deeply meditated the technique and the sound qualities of English poetry, and that his influence, had he lived to impose his voice on the public, would have been all to the good.

Much of his diction appears at first sight to be tired out, in fact to be just what needed renewing in English poetry, and yet his personal tone gives it a mysterious vigour. Seamus Heaney remarked in his essay 'The God in the Tree', on early Irish nature poetry (reprinted in *Preoccupations* 1980, p. 186), to which the nature poetry of Edward Thomas has a certain distant affinity, that "Poetry of any power is always deeper than its declared meaning. The secret between the words, the binding element, is often a psychic force which is elusive, archaic and only half-apprehended by maker and audience". Edward Thomas had considered and constantly re-experienced natural things until they had become profound elements in his imagination, deep metaphors for unexpressed feelings. He was also a naturalist, but that is another matter. In his two years or so of writing poetry, from late 1914 to late 1916, he handled that material with authority, and many of his poems have the same mysterious strength of which Seamus Heaney was speaking. It is not identical with nature mysticism or poetic pantheism; it has something to do with the expression of a self that was already deeply implicated in these images.

But as always with true poetry, there is also skill. His skill appears in the very first poem, 'Up in the Wind'. It is too long, it foolishly challenges comparison with Hardy, and it has a pale, middle class quality like that of most early Frost poems. But it has deeper notes and a few thrilling lines, and above all it has that inward life that comes from rhythm and momentum. Its inner meaning is darker than may appear. One can criticize details, such as the yodelling of the stone-curlew. That may be accurate, but it appeals to no common experience: it awkwardly imparts information no one needed. I am not sure how a stone-curlew differs from a curlew in note or habit; reference books confine it to the extreme south-east and I have never consciously seen or heard one; its usual cry is said to be like a common curlew's. A normal curlew's cry is unforgettable, though it is nothing like yodelling. The endemic fault of nature poetry is that it tends to become overladen, and the poetry somehow fails to absorb its own details. That was a fault Edward Thomas eliminated as time went by.

We have two versions of the short poem called 'A Tale'. The datum of this poem occurs in prose, dated in March 1915. "Outside the [old] ruined cottage is periwinkle and when that is not flowering there is some blue and white peering among the leaves." In the first version of the poem the careful bit of natural observation is made more "poetic", and several lines are overloaded with the merely beautiful.

> There once the walls
> Of the ruined cottage stood.

The periwinkle crawls
With flowers in its hair into the wood.

In flowerless hours
Never will the bank fail,
With everlasting flowers
On fragments of blue plates, to tell the tale.

The second version is a great deal colder. The meaning clarifies, and that hollow sound behind the words which is typical of Edward Thomas is more clearly heard. He loses nothing except the fanciful image in the fourth line of the first stanza, and the cottage is suddenly a real presence. In the early version, the question arose what a ruined cottage would be like if it had no walls. Now they are simply ruined.

Here once flint walls,
Pump, orchard and wood pile stood.
Blue periwinkle crawls
From the lost garden down into the wood.

The flowerless hours
Of Winter cannot prevail
To blight these other flowers,
Blue china fragments scattered, that tell the tale.

This is not a major poem, it is hardly more than an epigram. The contrast of the blue flowers and the blue china does not quite work as it was meant to work. The "flowerless hours" suggest a cockney rhyme in Keats's worst taste. The "cannot" in line six should probably read as "can't". And yet the very bareness of the barest statement in the second version says something beyond what the words say. Its first stanza is masterly, and the second is at least effective. And there are no other poems like it. Its subject-matter has not been reworked from other literature, nor has it been exhausted in explanation. It remains mysterious. Beyond the images lies a metaphor certainly, but a metaphor for what? Not just for the untold tale, but for some underlying truth or balance of feelings about life, of which I do not think Edward Thomas was quite fully conscious. He was not quite sure of the meanings he had invested in all these images, and perhaps no amount of mere explication would quite arrive at them. His poems expressed a self that had matured inaccessible to him before he began to write poetry. His case is in fact unique among English poets, in that ample material has built up a full biography of that self, which we know in some ways better than he knew himself, but what the poetry reveals is something deeper and more intimate, which biography in no way explains. Biography does not explain the poetry, but only to some considerable degree the self that the poetry expresses. In this fact lies a more general lesson about the biographies of poets, sharpened by the unique case of Edward Thomas.

His work foreshadowed the later achievements of others. His travel writing aided the regeneration of English topographic prose in the next generation. His antiquarian and naturalist observations lay down a line that has been profitably followed. His book on *Feminine Influence on the Poets* (1910) pointed towards *The White Goddess* and beyond, particularly in its fourth chapter 'Women, Nature and Poetry'. In other ways his work looks towards that of Geoffrey Grigson. He was a lonely man, belonging to no general movement, though he does of course reflect a general climate. None of his friends at Oxford are nowadays of any interest at all to us. St. Paul's and Oxford cut him off from the working class origins of his lower middle class family, and yet some spark of Welshness lived in him, and it may well be that a Welsh sense of sound-values runs through all his poetry. The Artists' Rifles in which he enlisted were a territorial unit intended to train officers; had Edward Thomas been working class he might have served in a London Welsh New Army battalion with David Jones, and died perhaps a year earlier. But his last diary is very fully expressive of him. It is among the most moving records of its kind.

I do not think his father's kind of positivism and the Church of Humanity, gruesome or ridiculous as they may seem today, did him any more harm than the equivalent brand of orthodox piety would have done. Jefferies and Father Faber have in common an uncontrolled emotional surge that masquerades as a philosophy of life. The long walks and the canal fishing of his boyhood are normal enough; it was not his wanderings that made him unhappy. His character was deep and to my mind fascinating, and his talent and willpower extraordinary. Poetry was not exactly a therapy to him, or he would have discovered it earlier. I do not think he can be called a self-indulgent poet; by 1914 no one called his personal maturity into question except his appalling old father. A brilliant critic might deduce from his verse the long prose training he underwent, but I doubt if even Robert Frost could have deduced from his prose, for all its cadences and moments of beauty, his high quality as a poet. Had he lived, I believe his reputation as a poet would have kept pace or more with Walter De La Mare and Robert Frost's.

I wish more could be made of his addiction to genuine ballads, but it shows some tact that he never wrote, or at least never sought to preserve any false ballads of his own. The linguistic purity and deadly accuracy, and the authentic poetry of the traditional ballads, have scarcely flourished in modern times except in lesser imitations of the same. European writers in less developed societies than ours, such as Lorca, Gatsos and Vasko Popa, have found solid foundations for modern literature in the ballads of their own languages, and I have the impression that Edward Thomas once aspired to do the same. Robert Graves and his sister went round Wales before the 1914 war collecting folk songs on a machine that used a wax cylinder, but alas nothing remains of the result, due to mechanical failure. It is fascinating that even Pound's bold attempt at the medieval ballad was comparatively speaking an embarrassing failure, and that only Eliot succeeded in using such powerful lines, by constructing an utterly new context for them. Yet Edward Thomas was in a good position to explore the relations between music and language. In time I believe he would have got round to doing so. In that area almost everything in the Modernist movement still useful to writers lies awaiting recovery. I take the relationship of music to 'The Trumpet' and 'Lights Out' to be merely suggestive, a matter of mood.

The secret of style in the poetry of Edward Thomas is the use of an individuated vernacular speech tone in descant with conventional metre and with itself. The conventional metre includes a certain amount of archaic construction and even diction. The result is an enlivened, springing line at which several Georgian poets aimed, but which few achieved, and maybe none so consistently, though I think someone ought to reread the work of John Drinkwater from this point of view. There is no doubt that Robert Frost was the master of that particular bag of tricks. "There's that cat got in. You get out you cat. But she'll be right back." Frost was brilliant in pointing out the moments when rhythmic life invaded the dead-looking verses of the past. It is likely enough that this subject was part of his endless conversations about poetry with Edward Thomas, in which it is probable that each taught the other. If I seem to be too heavy-footed in search of these flattening explanations, that is because the phenomenon of Edward Thomas and his individuality as a poet is so wonderful and so unexplained.

JOHN BAYLEY

The Self in the Poem

The Self in the Poem

To begin with 'Adlestrop' might seem banal. And yet that much anthologised poem does tell us a lot about Thomas. It is indeed, in its own peculiar sense, about Thomas. No poet better exemplifies the truth in T.S. Eliot's dictum that "no artist produces great art by a deliberate attempt to express his own personality", and yet Thomas, like Eliot himself, is in some essential sense the subject of his own poetry.

The same sense in which this is so might seem to be a distinctively English one. Neither Thomas nor Eliot are particularly 'English', except by private and personal inclination, and in their feel for what the English language can do as poetry. In the case of Thomas a poet's syntax is the expression, in some inevitably ambiguous sense, of the deepest and stillest nature of his being, not of what he wants to say, as "a man speaking to men", nor of the way he wants his poem to succeed, but as his way of finding, and being, himself in poetry.

As the excellent biography *Edward Thomas: A Portrait* (1985) by R. George Thomas makes clear, the influence and inspiration for Thomas of Robert Frost's visit to England was more important even than had been previously supposed. Thomas found he could unburden himself entirely to Frost, as an American, a poet, a man of understanding and sympathy unique in this context, as he could not to any of his friends, or to his wife. Frost, whose sympathy and intuition were remarkable, was even to offer to take Thomas's son Merfyn, with whom his father had been unable to get on, back to America with him. Apart from this service to his friend's morale Frost's example showed Thomas what might be done with his own special feeling for English locality, the feeling which up to then had only found utterance in essays, descriptive sketches and 'Nature Notes', and in the biography of Richard Jefferies. But as Frost's own much later poem, 'A Nature Note', was to make clear, something much more positive might be done: a break-through in vision or style could turn these things into a new sort of poetry.

This was what Frost had already achieved in his two collections, *A Boy's Will* (1913) and *North of Boston* (1914). The two photographs reproduced in R. George Thomas's book make a striking contrast. The grainy photo of Thomas at this time shows his handsome half profile and fine eyes set in a concentration of misery so deep that it must have frightened whoever held the camera. With two books already written Frost looks in his fresh candid way entirely pleased with himself, with his poetry, his status and his future. There is nothing invidious about this: Frost found early and completely the way to be himself in his new style; and there is what can only be called a wonderfully *comfortable* note, of something having been 'scored' for himself (Frost's own word) in those memorable poems which tell of swinging on birchtrees, or stopping by woods on a snowy evening, or the dream in the fact of haymaking, or having a lover's quarrel with the world.

Nothing less like Thomas's way of being and discovering himself can be imagined. Yet the breakthrough, though it went in an unexpected direction, came from Frost's example. In a letter to his friend Thomas refers, with a wry and affectionate humour, to what he calls "North of Bostonism".

> Sometimes brief unstrained impressions of things lately seen, like a drover with six newly shorn sheep in a line across a cool woody road on a market morning and me looking back to envy him and him looking back at me for some reason which I can't speculate on. Is this North of Bostonism?

Perhaps it was, yet it was also something that was to lead Thomas out of his real path. Admirable as his own version of "North of Bostonism" may be it is not the true Thomas, the Thomas who, without Frost's deliberate intention, made a special niche for himself, his own unmistakable kind of poetic sensibility. That is always the simple yet the effective criterion. The poet who adds a new world to our experience — as Auden does, as Larkin does — is for that reason the kind of poet who really counts. Such a poet is naturally unaware of what he is doing because he is becoming himself in his poetry, his true and involuntary self, not *making* and remaking himself, by the poetic will, as Yeats did, and as Frost did. Yeats and Frost are great poets of course, but their greatness is of a quite different kind. They do not bring a new sort of poetic world, the world of themselves, involuntarily into being.

Neither did Thomas when he was trying out his own version of "North of Bostonism", as he does for instance in 'The Chalk Pit' or 'As the team's head brass'. These are comparatively 'mature' poems: the Frost note and the Frost narrative are still more marked in Thomas's first poem, 'Up in the Wind', his most literal attempt at "North of Bostonism". Such poems have great qualities, but they could have been written by other poets; more than that, they give the impression of the poet working like a craftsman in a purely external medium, as Thomas wrote his reviews, essays and country sketches. In 'March' Thomas follows out Frost's advice that he should attempt a kind of verse based on the prose of his book of rural life, *In Pursuit of Spring*, which came out in 1914. It is a beautiful poem, and explores with all the accuracy of observation Thomas could do so well — better than Frost in his own way — the fact of spring coming and not coming in England, and how the thrushes have to cram an hour's frenzied singing between the hailstorms and the coming of night. But this brings us to 'Adlestrop', also a comparatively early poem, in which something quite different is happening. Its haunting quality, an elusive sense of personality fulfilled and come to fruition at last in its own disappearance, is Thomas's special trademark. We have that haunting in many other poems, early and late, in 'Tall Nettles', in 'It Rains', and most explicitly at the end of 'Lights Out'.

> The tall forest towers:
> Its cloudy foliage lowers
> Ahead, shelf above shelf:
> In silence I hear and obey
> That I may lose my way
> And myself.

Many such poems, like 'Old Man', started as a prose account or description, in which 'I' is paramount, and is carried over into the genesis of the poem. A function of the poem could then be said to be the final disappearance of the 'I'. The effect is the exact opposite of the many poems of Frost's in which a happening is developed by the poem and rounded off by the confirmed presence of himself, which it confers, as a poem, on the author. In 'Lights Out' the 'I' is present at the end of the poem, but present only in the imminence of extinction, disappearance. In the other poems the same effect is achieved not by statement but by the way the poem itself works. In the second stanza of 'Tall Nettles' the poet's presence and preference is occluded by the unusual and ambiguous syntax, brought about by the force of the colon.

> This corner of the farmyard I like most:
> As well as any bloom upon a flower
> I like the dust on the nettles, never lost
> Except to prove the sweetness of a shower.

The significance comes in the difference between the first and the second 'I' — the first emphatic and expansive, stating its feeling, the second merged and obscured by the presence of the weeds themselves, and the dust on them. Their own cycle of hours and days completely takes over the poem and its author, and one aspect of the poem's success, and of our enjoyment of it, is our awareness of the poet's thankfulness in going. He has realised himself in the poem by means of his own removal from it.

Syntax aids the process. The reader's eye is at first inclined to run over the word "most" and attach it to the second line. There is a slight shock when the reader realises how complete is the pause; unexpected in a poem of this form and length. The conversational, arhythmic tone of the third line, to an ear expecting a more conventional poetic movement and inclined at first to read it into the line ("I like the dust upon the néttles") has the same effect of removing the poet as poet. In 'Adlestrop' the effect is even more marked, and it is clear that Thomas in his early and experimental poems took particular care over it, playing off the acoustic roughness and jerkiness of punctuation and sentence structure against the formal arrangement of the stanzas. The punctuation variants recorded in R. George Thomas's edition indicate this, and there seems no doubt that Thomas finally decided on the full stop after the first word of the poem. "Yes". The pattern of speech dismisses the rural charm of the name (which has made it so much remembered in anthologies) almost instantly. The name is put to one side by the oncoming experience, in the same way that the poet himself, and his speech, will be, in the last stanza, by the singing of the birds. Adlestrop the place remains a blank, a fact emphasised in Thomas's first and second drafts by the phrase "At least the name". In becoming simply "the name", Adlestrop adds to the indefinably memorable and yet casual nature of what occurs there. What happened has too the deepest sadness of things in it, a fact which must very likely have been noted by Walter De La Mare, some of whose own best poems give the same impression, though without any of the same peculiar accuracy, an accuracy which is both comforting and desolating. De La Mare, like Thomas, was not at home in the world which both saw with such a subdued intensity.

The strange sadness of the poem goes with the comedy of its name. And with the tone with which the subject is introduced. In 'Church Going' Philip Larkin brings something of the same kind of comedy to what is for him a very significant internal experience — "tense, musty, unignorable". Yet it is an experience which has its comically absurd and touching side, as probably all our most intimate personal experiences do.

> Hatless, I take off
> My cycle-clips in awkward reverence,
>
> Move forward, run my hand around the font.
> From where I stand, the roof looks almost new –
> Cleaned, or restored? Someone would know: I don't.

Taking off one's cycle-clips because unable to make the gesture of removing a hat is a piece of invisible comedy which would have appealed to Thomas, as would the words and pauses (the comma after "where I stand") in which Larkin recounts his experience. The way poets 'notice such things' is itself equivocal, as Larkin dryly commented about Hardy, who could — as he pointed out — with equal if not greater honesty have written a poem about someone who used to notice nothing at all. All noticings are selective, itself a topic for droll incongruities. Larkin, the obsessive church-goer, notices out of complete ignorance (but the ignorance is fed by something "unignorable") and Larkin must have spoken for many of us when he remarked to John Betjeman that "churches were all the same". The truth of the comment was perhaps acknowledged in the amiable way in which the expert replied: "I wouldn't quite say that".

Certain kinds of experience are "all the same". That is somehow acknowledged too in the tone and depth of 'Adlestrop'. The poet is not claiming the special intensity of an 'epiphany', with its implicit claim to a personal specialness (that specialness which hovers over every short successful poem of Frost's). The experience of 'Adlestrop' could and has happened to everybody, which explains the popularity of the poem, and the way we at once recognise the experience, though unable to formulate it as the poet has done. Thomas's diary entries, on which the poem is based, are of course more diluted, indicating a chain of experiences rather than the single minute which makes up the poem; and they, and its variants, show the economy with which the poem simplifies the contrasts in its own being.

> ...we stopped at Adlestrop, through the willows could be heard a chain of blackbirds' songs at 12.45 and one thrush and no man seen, only a hiss of engine letting off steam. Stopping outside Campden by banks of long grass, willowherb and meadowsweet, extraordinary silence between two periods of travel — looking out on grey dry stones between metals and the shining metals and over it all the elms, willows and long grass — one man clears his throat — a greater than rustic silence, No house in view. Stop only for a minute till signal is up.

The ingredients are all there, but jostling each other and leading up to no special blessing of vacancy, as they do at the poem's ending, in which both the poet and his observations seem to disappear. In the poem the silence created by the man who clears his throat comes together with the hiss of steam, and the vacancy of the platform. More important, the poem gets rid of the emphasis with which the poet of the diary entries noted his observation of the contrasts. This survived in Thomas's original draft for the third stanza.

> And willows, willow herb and grass,
> And meadowsweet. The haycocks dry
> Were not less still
> Than the high cloud tiers in the sky.

In the completed poem that stanza, like the last one, abandons the short choppy sentence structure of the first two, preparing for the enveloping stillness which succeeds the contrasts. The full stop is taken out; the grass, flowers and hay united, as it were, with the stillness of "the high cloudlets in the sky". So that the final, and deepest, contrast in the poem, one not noticed in the diary entries, is also the most diminishing, the least 'noticed'.

> And for that minute a blackbird sang
> Close by, and round him, mistier,

Farther and farther, all the birds
Of Oxfordshire and Gloucestershire.

The single blackbird is answered by others farther off, diminishing into ghost song in the still distance, the dream-like borders of two counties; Gloucestershire, the last named, giving something like the song itself in the separate and liquid notes of its spoken and written form.

Diminishment of perspective into nothing is a seduction that Thomas explores early in his poetry, perhaps first in 'Old Man', about "The hoar-green feathery herb, almost a tree,/ Growing with rosemary and lavender." which is also based on a prose version. The poem, however, produces its own kind of end, one that shows how the new self of Thomas in his poetry came into being when, in 1914, the poems "began to run". 'Old Man' is a kind of reverse image of what was happening to Thomas himself, as he found himself in his poetry. The bitter scent of the herb reminds him of nothing; yet it seems to be the scent, as it were, of memory itself; and memory is close to, and closes in, oblivion.

I sniff the spray
And think of nothing; I see and I hear nothing;
Yet seem, too, to be listening, lying in wait
For what I should, yet never can, remember:
No garden appears, no path, no hoar-green bush
Of Lad's-love, or Old Man, no child beside,
Neither father nor mother, nor any playmate;
Only an avenue, dark, nameless, without end.

The strange thing about the poem, as about a good few of Thomas's, is that from its very negative self such a positive image of the poet should be beginning to emerge. The need to be a poet was also the need for oblivion, the two at least lying close to each other. In the same days of early December 1914, if R. George Thomas's painstaking detection work is correct, and I am sure it is, Thomas also wrote 'The Other', an equally strange but this time unsuccessful poem, in which the sense of himself forming into poetry (the "hoar-green feathery herb" ceasing to be a mere nature note or anecdote, and becoming a potent image of self experience) is expressed in the melodramatic form of the Other (or *Doppelgänger*), the detached self who follows or is followed by his double, from whom he can never escape.

I steal out of the wood to light;
I see the swift shoot from the rafter
By the inn door: ere I alight
I wait and hear the starlings wheeze
And nibble like ducks: I wait his flight.
He goes: I follow: no release

> Until he ceases. Then I also shall cease.

Thomas's instinct for the right word and cadence, which was also the unexpected one, was already strong, as is shown by his use of the word "also" in the last line of the poem, instead of "too". But the idea of the Other is too crudely explicit, not at all his "style", as if he had picked it up from some alien literary source, which indeed he very probably had. 'The Other' renders a preoccupation far too explicit, so that it seems to belong to someone else, or be a conceit that any writer might have. Going with this is the crude way in which 'noticings' — the starlings' grotesque sounds, beautifully caught, and the shoot of the swift — are tacked on to the poem rather than having essential kinship with its self.

I would say that Thomas, like Larkin, apprehends experience other than his own very keenly, yet it must none the less have some deep connection with his poetical self. In both writers purely 'objective' poems may be excellently done, but lack the individuality of the inner life. Thomas rapidly became adept at melding together his sense of things with that of his own internal and undeclared being; and always the most haunting effect is that elusive sense of a personality, like 'The Unknown Bird'of his poem, offering a brief glimpse before being fulfilled in its own, and the poem's, and its subject's, disappearance. 'The Path' is in this way a much more memorable and potent image than 'The Other'. The path must be frequented by children, who have worn away the thin moss that tries to grow there.

> But the road is houseless, and leads not to school.
> To see a child is rare there, and the eye
> Has but the road, the wood that overhangs
> And underyawns it, and the path that looks
> As if it led on to some legendary
> Or fancied place where men have wished to go
> And stay; till, sudden, it ends where the wood ends.

So mesmerically vivid is the glimpse that one feels one knows the very place that Thomas is talking about, the raised path beside a road in a beechwood that "overhangs/ And underyawns it". And this sense of knowing is like knowing the poet himself, and ends equally abruptly. There is a faint irony, of which the poet is fully conscious, in the notion that the path leads "to some legendary/ Or fancied place where men have wished to go/ And stay". No such place exists. And the word "stay" reminds us of that, and of Thomas's own very personal and very subtle sense of disenchantment, a kind that is miles away from the old commonplace of romantic poetry, where "the fancy cannot cheat so well/ As she is feigned to do". And yet of course there is a connection.

The poems rarely end on any notion of 'uplift'. That is to be expected, and a part of their sudden expression of Thomas's own very deep and prolonged dissatisfactions with life, dissatisfactions more compelling and in a way more deserved — more *earned* — than those which in Hardy's poems are much more obviously on display. It is illuminating to compare what seems the real self of Thomas in such poems as 'The Path', 'The Ash Grove', and 'It Rains', with a more obviously 'poetic' attempt like 'The Barn', or 'Sedge-Warblers'. Not only do 'noticings' stick out too much in the latter poems, but something very much like a conventional moral of the time is drawn in them, a moral which fits too evidently with the mores of the Georgian literary scene, and with Thomas's communings with other poets of the time. The beauty of the summertime river in 'Sedge-Warblers' suggests to the poet an ideal beauty

divine and feminine,
Child of the sun, whose happy soul unstained
Could love all day, and never hate or tire,
Lover of mortal or immortal kin.

Syntax, vocabulary and rhythm are all of the time rather than of Thomas himself, and so is the 'lesson' in the poem, which is that the reality of things is sweeter than any dream of them, dreams which in their nature are 'poisonous', because producing disillusions that distract men from the true being of nature. "The fact is the sweetest dream that labor knows", as Frost's poem 'Mowing' puts it. The sedge-warblers have only a small monotonous song, lacking "all words, all melody", but this is what Thomas says is for him "the best of May" —

the small brown birds
Wisely reiterating endlessly
What no man learnt yet, in or out of school.

Thomas says so, but do we quite believe him? A distinction must be drawn between the charm and warmth of the friend, for which so much heartfelt evidence was given by his own friends; the man whose speaking voice, whether reading poetry or simply talking, was so beautiful that they said he would have made a wonderful preacher; and the solitary man for whom a certain kind of utterance in poetry had become an inner compulsion. 'The Path' is a very different kind of poem from 'Sedge-Warblers', although there is a similarity in what both poems are saying (or in the case of 'The Path' implying) about the difference between what we dream or fancy about the world of nature, and what is really going on in it. The difference is between a comparatively public poem and a private one ('The Path'),and Thomas's best, most characteristic, poetry is inherently private.

Moreover "it ends where the wood ends", like the path. His best poems do not leave a message with us, as Wordsworth's, for instance, might be said to do, but take a sudden departure, as if returning into a self whose truest expression is its own wish for non-existence — to end with the path, with the scent of Lad's Love, with the dead trees of 'The Ash Grove' where

> Not even the spirits of memory and fear with restless wing,
> Could climb down in to molest me over the wall
>
> That I passed through at either end without noticing.

Thomas wrote no love poems. The 'household poems' to his wife and children are almost unbearably public, as if something hidden and sardonic in him were laying on a display of rustic appropriateness, a kind of concert at the village hall. The parade of quaint English place names has no such function as that which gives its subtle humour to 'Adlestrop'. Only at the end of the poem to Helen does there emerge sentiment unusual in a love poem, but going to the heart of the matter. He wishes many good things for her — "All kinds of loveliness and truth" — and ends

> And myself, too, if I could find
> Where it lay hidden and it proved kind.

These words, to borrow a line of Larkin's, are "not untrue and not unkind", but their import would be chilling, none the less. Thomas has found his self in his poetry, but it is not a self that his wife and family, or even his friends, could share. To them it must necessarily remain undeclared: it is declared only to the anonymous reader, whose solitary intimacy with Thomas extends to his awareness of the poem, and no farther.

In a review of the Imagist poets, appearing in 1914, Thomas remarked that these poets, and Pound in particular, had found a way of avoiding "any commonplaces of verse" by sounding like a translation. It is a shrewd point, one of the many shrewd ones assembled by Edna Longley in her excellent anthology of Thomas's criticism, *A language not to be betrayed* (1981). Her title is a phrase used by Thomas himself, and the two comments — as is so often the way with Thomas — have a subterranean life together. Thomas knew how much ordinary poetry is indeed betrayed by its language, just as he knew how swiftly and inexorably verse sets up its own form of commonplace. His own way of avoiding the commonplace, as of avoiding self-betrayal, was by becoming in poetry the sort of man he really was.

Thomas's best and most characteristic poetry, therefore, is as far from that of his contemporary Georgians as it is from the Modernists who succeeded after the war. Bizarre as it may seem, the poet he most resembles, in terms of temperament, and the outlet his talent found, is probably A.E. Housman, the Housman who poured out the poems that make up *A Shropshire Lad* as a result of his unhappy love for a fellow undergraduate, Moses Jackson, and a second harvest of poems when Jackson died. Nothing so dramatic and so personal as this in the case of Thomas: and yet the feeling of a life that has gone wrong, and cannot say why, finding at length a mode of utterance that becomes its own sadness and its own solace, both unique to this poet, is the impression his poems leave upon us. Had he survived the war he might well have plunged himself wholly, as Housman did, into some quite other activity, because there was nothing of the professional poet about him; but later, for some reason hardly suspected by the reader, or by his own friends, perhaps not even by the poet himself, the poems must surely have started to 'run' again.

J.P. WARD

The Solitary Note: Edward Thomas and Modernism

The Solitary Note: Edward Thomas and Modernism

In the passage from *The Icknield Way* (1913) on which the poem 'Rain' was based Edward Thomas writes: "Once I heard through the rain a bird's questioning watery cry — once only and suddenly. It seemed content, and the solitary note brought up against me the order of nature, all its beauty, exuberance and everlastingness like an accusation. I am not a part of nature...". That Thomas so feels he *is* a part of nature, in other places in his work, accounts perhaps for the ambiguities he feels and expresses, the sweetness of his melancholy, the uncertainty about solitude itself ("so that if I feared the solitude,/ far more I feared all company...") and provides for the tension needed at any powerful poetry's core. Yet the note of the solitary itself, however it be dealt with, is ubiquitous in Thomas's poetry, and it is its compulsive expression — the way the rain itself, for example, in the poem referred to, as well as the bird's cry in the prose passage, that repeatedly yet with subtle diversity patters — that seems most to distinguish Thomas from the Modernism of the contemporary group that included Eliot and Pound. Both linguistically and humanly the solitary note separates him, as does its diversification; that entailing no contradiction, since when a mode of writing works in a narrow range throughout yet still retains our attention, it is likely that variations are being played of a very subtle order indeed. This very narrowness rebounds, at least narrowly, in Thomas's favour, as much as to say that if we concentrate *here* our interest must all the more be compelled by the very act and mood of expression undistracted.

The point, if true, is surely important for what it says about a theory currently prevalent in English criticism, the view that Pound and Eliot made innovations that led to, if not a cul-de-sac, then certainly a detour (the terms are Graham Hough's) in English poetry, a detour that with and since the 'fifties has rejoined the main line. The English line, on this legitimate if over-simplified view, is exemplified by Chaucer and Shakespeare certainly, but more directly so in Herbert, Wordsworth, Clare and Hardy, is finally characterized by the presence of a quiet personal voice rather than a public one, and is most deeply concerned with the individual mind and mood in the ethos of not the metaphysical or urban but the natural and domestic. It peters out with the Georgians, and even if it had not would have needed the blood-transfusion of Symbolism and Imagism to cope adequately with the new sensibilities engendered by the internationalism, technology, epistemological uncertainties, new plastic arts and new social orders of our world. But Modernist poetry is concerned with the solitary least of anything, and it is this fact that most discounts any remote claim (not that it has ever been made) for any identity between Thomas and the Modernist movement. Unfortunately, until recently, such identification for Thomas has too often been made at the other extreme, with the orthodox Georgians. His distinctiveness from that very different group however is clear from even the quickest reading of them, and itself argues Thomas's importance in understanding the course of this 'English line' and the place of Pound and Eliot next to it. The Georgians were *not* descendants of that line, certainly not in their practice. Reading De La Mare, Flecker, Masefield and the rest, one notices most a near-absence of interest in much beyond poem-making itself. They seem to have no psychological or social interests, no root in nature, religion or myth, neither radicalism nor a communally-rooted conservatism, and little self-awareness. It is paradoxically an argument for the genuineness of their claim to be poets that the poetic sonority they were left with should then be compulsively pushed to its limits. I can enjoy Flecker —

> And thou shalt sell thy wares for thrice the Damascene retailers' price,
> And buy a fat Armenian slave who smelleth odorous and nice.

— without feeling any underpinning of my existence, or exuberance or sadness in it, at the heart of the twentieth century. But it is the uncompromising self-effacing of Thomas's poetry, its bleakness and rhythmically captured tentativity, its intrigue with the elusive and half-seen in the barest language possible — the language of the solitary, not of external artefacts or exotic cultures (Armenian, USURA, "sneezing is a cure for hiccough", *che sublia es laissa cader* or whatever) but of mind's very morphology itself — that connects Clare and Hardy to a perhaps at first sight unlikely tradition to follow, that of Kafka, Beckett and Pinter, as well as the Movement poets. (To me at least, Donald Davie's silence on any place of Thomas, in Davie's *Thomas Hardy and British Poetry* (1973) or his books on the poetic resilience of syntax, is extraordinary.) Thomas, without the hopelessness, hell or nightmare of at least some of these, makes a similarly stripped-down verbal confrontation with reality in a world where the objective is not 'imitated' by an equally solid, traditionally-sanctioned, rich language.

In short then, there are two reactions to the Georgians, not one. There is that of Modernism, Imagism, Eliot and Pound, and there is that of the bleaker existentialists, even Wittgensteinians, those who would courageously strip language itself back to its own structure, its bare bones, distrustful of the succulence of rich nominal vocabularies, metaphor and physical imagery. They are left with themselves and their voices. And it is poetry as voice rather than artifice that can express mood, the response to the threat of the lonely world; it *must* require precisely that "enthusiastic personal direction of the phrase" to which Mallarmé denied poetic validity.

Why Thomas so needed to write the poetry of voice (and in his case of 'whisper', as he called it) I hope to suggest. But first it is clear that this prevented any espousal of Modernism which, having as one of its deliberate aims that of violating expectation, would not at all object to using words outside of their place in speech. Since Modernism is also overtly and programmatically concerned with all art forms, and the totality of art, for its poetry to use techniques from sculpture or the visual arts is equally to be expected. Finally, since the freedom that the Modernist modes of poetry allow to themselves removes all barriers to the use of avalanches of words from any language or culture (accounting in *The Cantos* and *The Waste Land* for the ransacking of any likely effective, surprising, deranging resource), so all the more is the individual speaking mood obviated as a possible poetic attitude. There is thus little *voice* heard or echoing from much Symbolist or Imagist poetry unless, as in *The Waste Land*, several *personae* speak dramatically with the result of a unity that must still nonetheless transcend any individual, overheard, inner mood in the same way. Certainly there is a strong voice, sad and wearied, in *Prufrock* and *Four Quartets*, and recent biographical studies have shown where this came from. But the voice was always an attitude to the external materials of diversified civilisation. One could never think of Eliot that the voice was coterminous with the poetry itself. Whereas Thomas's voice is inescapably that of one man and the poetry is inextricably bound to that and imprisoned by it.

But, most important of all, if no human mouth, thought or emotion is conceived of as actually occasioning, even constituting, the poem on the page, then it follows that the words themselves are being seen as autonomous, near-tangible material and substance, which the poet does not so much utter to capture an emotional inner rhythm, but which he uses more as external material, more like clay or wood, even if 'musically' at another level. Much Modernist poetry, not necessarily inhuman or dead, feels as though it has been worked from the outside. (Thus T.E. Hulme's moon like a "red-faced farmer" seems to *be* the poem, whereas Thomas's overt images — and they are rare — are themselves inseparable from the mood of the poet, so that the "grasshopper [that] works at his sewing-machine/ So hard" and the poet's own "right hand/ Crawling crab-like over the clean white page" give us not only those pictures but the poet's wistfulness toward them.) In short the Modernist interest lies precisely in being aesthetically self-conscious, looking at language to see its intrinsic characteristics and potential as though for the first time, detaching it from its human and communal base and thus considering new, hitherto unthought-of possibilities. And of course a vast amount of Pound's cajolings and exhortations to his fellow-poets were on these questions of technique seen impersonally. There is no moody confession of the kind found when the poet's work is more nearly synonymous with his life. Such gentle mood can only be practised by taking the language of it for granted — by assuming in fact "A language not to be betrayed", that line of Thomas which his admirers and critics find so quotable when they try to pin down his heart concerns — instead of, on the contrary, always "making it new".

And this Modernism, in Britain at least, swung into full view at almost exactly the time Thomas was beginning to write poetry or wondering whether to write poetry. Pound came to London in 1908; Frost came, and met Edward Thomas, in 1913. Thomas's affinity with the mode of Robert Frost is undeniable and is not affected by the evidence we have that Frost and Thomas did not influence each other poetically so much as give each other encouragement. They did not need to influence each other poetically; the similarities of linguistic interest existed independently. (Whereas aside from the enthusiastic review by Thomas in 1909 of *Personae*, recanted almost immediately afterwards, the sum of his attitude to this school is the single reference in his letters to Gordon Bottomley, "What imbeciles the Imagists are".) The question therefore arises of how far, not a Modernist in any strict sense, Thomas can be an important twentieth century poet at all, how far he may express a "distinctively modern sensibility" as Leavis put it in *New Bearings in English Poetry* (1932), if, as Modernists' supporters claim, it is Modernist experiments alone that could capture and have authentic place in the deranged, uncertain secular world. As is well known many critics hold exactly that view of Modernism. Here is Frank Kermode: "Without [poetic decreation] poetry had no future we can now seriously conceive of." One need not deny the exhilarating influence of Imagism and Symbolism in poetry nor even, in hindsight, a certain inevitability about them, to find that a very extreme remark. However, such controversy is to do with the wider, still prevailing dispute as to whether, in a recent formulation, Modernism is indeed "the supreme modern expression" or merely "of marginal importance" (Malcom Bradbury and James McFarlane: *Modernism*, 1976). The immediate task is to see how Edward Thomas's mode, wholly incompatible with Modernism's tenets, expressed something with poetic inevitability, and therefore necessary to be expressed, in that same modern world.

If one throws off the spectacles that still reveal to some Thomas the 'Georgian', the 'nature poet', we see that at the most cursory level he had the attributes of a twentieth-century existentialist. He is privatized, inner and alienated; he is colloquial; he is concerned with poetry's and language's difficulty; he is secular (in religious terms he is neither believer, atheist nor agnostic). Most important, he seems free of the burden of reverence for the individual word of vast, historical, 'poetic', elevating associations. He does not use a wide vocabulary at all. He is wholly uninterested, as David Jones is interested, in resurrecting ancient words, or present words' ancient meanings. His attention is not on single words and their associations, their 'richness'. In this respect, as already suggested, he seems surprisingly close to the modes of Kafka and Beckett, and even Wittgensteinian philosophy. He uses the skeleton of language not its flesh, the wires and strings rather than what they join. It is as though at least one strand of modern urban sensibility does not need, perhaps cannot bear, the weight of too heavy a verbal heritage, and when the diminished — many would say impoverished — language is resultingly used it is often in fatigued or whimsical tone or even, as in Pinter, a sort of dumb expression of nothing, an utterance arrested. That is as may be. But it does seem that in our century the new self-consciousness towards words can go two ways. As with Thomas and the existentialists the word may slip away and go self-effacing, elided and thin, whereas with the Symbolists and Imagists the word, precisely through our decreasing sense of its everyday value, may all the more be detachable from human intercourse and thus usable as objective medium for art, for artifice. The way to the *parole-langue* distinction opens. Which of these two responses any poet took to the crisis of the word depended presumably on his sense of language at the moment of first poetic decision. What Thomas had to express necessitated for him the first of these two ways, a contention we can perhaps support by considering some of the ways in which he used it and their implications.

By trusting very directly the cadence of his own mind as it occurs in words on each occasion, Thomas was first able to produce lines of extraordinarily subtle and rippling cadence themselves. In this he was incidentally able to obey Hulme's dictum to capture "the exact curve of the thing" differently on each occasion in a way not envisaged by Hulme himself. (He also gave if not a heave, perhaps a small nudge, to the pentameter.) Thus the overt curve of lines like "And I am nearly as happy as possible", "A house that shall love me as I love it", and the little halt in an otherwise similar line "I love it, as some day the child shall love it". Against the clarity of such base-lines the force is felt of a truncation like "I am something like that" in 'Blenheim Oranges' where the writer seems suddenly to surprise and sober himself with his abrupt recognition that he is himself like the old house he is talking about. So much so that he repeats the line at the beginning of the next stanza too; "I am something like that", as though to try the line again, see whether it does indeed express adequately what he is feeling, whether it is true. In this sense his poetry is reflexive. It curls back on itself and the voice makes this possible. Something similar happens with "I could not love; I could not command love", as though the second phrase deliberately re-phrases the first, and rethinks it. All these lines, detached from context, scarcely seem to have been part of poems at all; their success therefore lies in their cumulative orchestration within whole poems and indeed within the entire body of Thomas's very homogeneous work; their incessant restriking, in fact, of the solitary note. That they are successful is confirmed by the experience they give us in reading, their integrity contrasting furthermore with the occasional lapse as in 'The Other' where the line "I quite forgot I could forget" sounds merely like a verbal trick and empty jingle. His cadences are seldom such jingles.

These cadences can work so single-mindedly, though still tentatively, precisely because they are not tied to a firm body of vocabulary representative of any objective, solid 'content' about which Thomas writes and which would amount to a duality of focus by distracting our attention from the voice itself. Certainly Thomas writes about 'nature', in a special way, but this is merged with the compulsion by which many lines direct their rhythm to something not finally said, to something half-verbalized and elusive. This has of course been repeatedly noticed about Thomas; it is inescapable. Again representative lines may be taken: "Maybe I should not count it anything...", "When last I heard it I cannot recall...", "In hope to find whatever it is I seek", and the many conditional clauses, the 'if'; "Sad more than joyful it was, if I must say/ That it was one or other, but if sad...". The general form "If...had been, then might I have..." is common in Thomas. But his willingness to leave the elusive entity as it is does not arise, it seems, from some congenital inability to pursue the ineffable to its finish. On the contrary, such straining after what he 'seeks' is at times the only justification for what might otherwise be merely cloying. Thus in 'Melancholy' — almost the prototype Thomas poem — his reference to that mood as of a "strange sweetness" and "soft as dulcimers" can work only because it is not an inert pair of poeticizing opposites but a contradiction left where it is, in order to capture, not so much some particular elusive thing, but his very feeling in the face of elusiveness itself. Furthermore there are contrasting strong lines in Thomas's poetry which in their clinching of the position he is left with are direct and often monosyllabic:

> And yet I still am half in love with pain.

The whole of the 'The Gallows' has this monosyllabic directness and certainty, so that the dead creatures' deadness is reinforced by their hanging "On the dead oak tree bough"; and that existentially rock-bottom line where the keeper, in shooting the thieving crow, "Made him one of the things that were" is an irreducibly satisfying touch that survives long after we might expect to forget it. So Thomas's absorption with the elusive, and in fact his acceptance of it, have a different basis. A clue to this seems to lie in one feature of his poems more than most; namely, his particular mode of repetition.

His particular mode of repetition is found in a very large number of his poems indeed. We have already said it is reflexive. It almost constitutes the movement of, for example, 'Old Man':

> Old Man, or Lad's-love, — in the name there's nothing
> To one that knows not Lad's-love, or Old Man,

Why not simply say 'them' the second time?

> Even to one that knows it well, the names
> Half decorate, half perplex, the thing it is:
> At least, what that is clings not to the names
> In spite of time. And yet I like the names.

"names", "half" and even "is" which by being stressed in the second case is in effect a repetition. He goes on:

> The herb itself I like not, but for certain
> I love it, as some day the child will love it.

The lines would make near-identical sense without the second "love it", yet the feeling would be missing of a re-cycling back to a point earlier left. Examples of single lines include "And what was hid should still be hid", "must I be content with discontent" (in the oddly Prufrockian ending to 'The Glory') and in 'The long small room' where "Only the moon, the mouse and the sparrow peeped" becomes "When I look back I am like" again not "them" but "moon, sparrow and mouse". Often passages of three or four lines in poems diversify pairs or trios of words in this way, and the feeling is very often of this cyclical kind. This curious compulsion, if that is what it is, comes markedly in 'Old Man', 'The Other', 'Parting', 'Health', 'Liberty', 'I never saw that land before', 'Melancholy', 'Home', 'The Word' and many other poems. The valency of these repetitions contrasts for instance Pound's "beauty is difficult" and his "bischniz", which act more as an insistent refrain, while in Thomas it is not at all refrain. Eliot's phrases seem more like Thomas in the *Four Quartets* but Eliot is then suddenly explicit about it:

> You say I am repeating
> Something I have said before. I shall say it again,
> Shall I say it again? In order to arrive there,
> To arrive where you are, to get from where you are not,
> You must go by a way wherein there is no ecstasy.
> In order to arrive at what you do not know
> You must go by a way which is the way of ignorance.

— and we quickly see that Eliot's repeats are amounting to a very public sort of litany, the curvature of cycling phrases achieving across the poem as a whole an outlined *pronunciamento*. With Thomas the repeated word or words seems a quiet, if melancholic reassurance. "Some day I shall think this a happy day", "till, sudden, it ends where the wood ends". To repeat it is to return to it and find it surviving.

I take it that these repeats express the finitude of a man's reaching and accepting the bounds of his own thinking, in a way analogous to repeat-phrases like "a sociology of sociology" and "the meaning of meaning" in more explicit disciplines. A barrier in intellectual penetration is reached so that, with nothing further to add, we start using the same words again, as though someone were to bump into an invisible perspex frame and begin to notice the doubling-up of his or her own footprints. Not that Thomas was on such an overt intellectual quest. Rather in a more rounded human way he trusts his copulative and skeletal language to find its own boundaries, to stop pushing outwards when the mind's rhythm ceases naturally to ask for it. He trusts the connection between language and mind, language and emotions. Again it is not that the Modernists distrust it but that they put language to an altogether different and new use. Thomas's cadences, ripples, monosyllabic irreducible lines, his drop-aways (so often, and surely rarely in poetry, to that word 'it'), his returning, recycling repetitions — all these as suggested, seem to mean a concern not to find *what* is elusive but rather to leave it so and therefore to capture the quality and feeling of elusiveness itself. Certainly he pursues, hesitates, and is sad, but this is not fear of the elusive itself. Rather, to find the unknown at the edge of the known and normal is itself wholly normal; the elusiveness is normal as is the melancholy it brings. To the austerely enquiring mind this is tame and tedious. As Pound said, the poet must learn to use his tools as sharply and exactly as he can: "a term must mean one particular thing...[otherwise] all metaphysical thought descends into soup. A soft terminology is merely an endless series of indefinable middles". That is wholly legitimate, and was arguably indeed the main challenge to poets at the start of this century. But if the very quality of the indefinable, of indefinableness itself, is what compels the poet's attention, then the twentieth-century poet will be thrown back not on language's treasure-chest but its action and structure, its inseparability from his mood and mind themselves. Thomas is nearer to Wittgenstein's precept, that "Whereof one cannot speak, thereof one must be silent". The difference with Thomas is that he would almost try to express that very silence; in his own term, as already said, to whisper. The meaning of this 'whispering' seems the final point to consider.

The two crucial poems on this matter, (both explicit about 'whispering'), 'Aspens' and 'I never saw that land before', seem to ask that we take his 'whispering' rather literally, as those sounds and half-noises, human but more likely natural, that do not resolve into actual words yet seem to articulate some meaning. In the first poem the "aspens at the cross-roads talk together" and in the second the breeze "hinted all and nothing spoke." The same theme is explicit in 'The Word', where the thrush's note utters "an empty thingless name" — "Some thrushes learn to say it as they sing." Thomas calls this "a pure thrush word", a more confident response than in 'Rain', where the rain's solitary note itself becomes very nearly but never quite the equivalent of a human or at least articulated cadence. This emphasis which runs through Thomas is curiously parallelled, though in more mischievous and sunlit fashion, in much of the earlier Wallace Stevens, with (as Kermode somewhere puts it of 'Harmonium'), his "birds and cries and odd little noises". It seems the subjective, neo-romantic counterpart to the much more explicit experiments of Modernism with the basis of language in actual sounds, phonemes themselves. But in 'Aspens' and 'I never saw that land before' Thomas seems to declare directly that these soft sounds (which occur also in 'Melancholy', "sounds of near water falling", then to become "Rumours") are a half-way point between man and nature itself. The sounds of rain, leaves, air, water and birds are the embryo of full articulation. Only one rung above them, perhaps imperceptibly coming out of them, are man's 'whispers', mutterings, half-suggested communications. It does not quite matter, at least at one level, whether we know exactly what was said ("I neither expected anything/ Not yet remembered"), what matters is that "some goal/ I touched then", and what also matters is not the content of the sentence so much as its cadence, its sound when we hear sound alone and, as Frost himself put it, "through a shut door or across a field". This, anathema to the Imagists, is wholly consistent with the interests of the age of linguistics and of the origin of language in the natural and human community.

It is then, oddly enough, the rooted community — the community, but as rooted in nature — which Thomas writes in and assumes. Here he parts company with Kafka and Beckett; though "Tired, angry, and ill at ease" he inhabits a sane natural world rather than one of lunar impossibility or mere nightmare, and it is the tension between this and the necessarily solitariness of the expression of it that seems Thomas's creative source. In correct New-Critical style I mentioned earlier his use of repetition, but could as easily, following the ideas of Lévi-Strauss, have written of repetition's use of Edward Thomas. Lévi-Strauss has suggested that when he uses his mind to describe myth among South American Indians, he is equally using the myth of South American Indians to reveal the structure of his own mind. Lévi-Strauss suggests also that the most profound, most fundamental expression of the structure and heart of a culture's mind is its music. That is human consciousness articulated but prior to words, the very form of consciousness itself. The suggestion then is that a concern for that rooting in immediate nature, a love of that, will engage the poet in a refining or singing of the voice that is a channel from physical nature, sound's source, and meaning-carrying words. The voice will have his attention, or be the expression of his attention. The Modernist poet on the contrary removes the words from the constraints of voice; he sets them free, and deliberately so, to become not nature but "hammered gold", the new Byzantium's artifice. Thomas's nature is very immediate indeed, he is down in it rather than astride mountains and contemplating huge landscapes; he writes of tall nettles and jam-jars set to catch wasps, and his answer, "Literally, for this" (when asked what he was fighting for in World War I) was accompanied not by a sweeping manual gesture to include wide plains and counties, but by taking a pinch of soil at his feet. Thus his roll-calls of names, often noted by critics as some object of attention, seem to me themselves to be part of his articulation. His lists of flowers, his "Codham, Cockridden and Childerditch", his recounting of the stages of Lob through English rural history, seem to present the names themselves, their sounds, as constitutive of the country of which and in which he is talking. I confess to finding it too pious an interpretation of 'Lob' to see in it a deliberate injunction to us to respect or adhere to some particular traditional value. That may result in the reader but not through that kind of persuasion. That is perhaps why so much of the poem 'Lob' is itself talk, itself the articulation of the trusted language. If simply trusting the language can produce so solitary a note as this poetry seems to — 'solitary' not only in the loneliness which so sadly tenses against the sociality implied by the voiced language, but solitary also in the singleness of voice of the result — then we can see in what sense even normally so analytical a critic as F.R. Leavis was content to leave it that Thomas's poems "seem to happen". Pound desired no such lack of contrivance.

ROBERT WELLS

Edward Thomas and England

Edward Thomas and England

I

Edward Thomas once described himself as "a lean indefinite man". The occasion is an encounter in *The Icknield Way*. He is on the road out of Dunstable one evening, gladly — or so he thinks — admiring the sweep of the Downs and the contrast of darkening earth and bright sky, when he falls in with "a philosopher who seemed to be equally moved yet could not decide whether his condition was to be described as happiness or melancholy". It is soon clear that this "philosopher" — the word is used with contemptuous irony — is Thomas himself, one of the many self-characterisations in his writing. The chapter is entitled 'Odsey to Edlesborough', and up to this point has consisted of straightforwardly descriptive travelogue. Now it lurches into poetic prose with an abrupt change of scene, as the philosopher tries inconsequentially to define the ambiguities of his mood. Place-names provide most of the chapter-headings in *The Icknield Way*, and suggest a steady passage by stages along the ancient route. But an earlier chapter, given over to an attempt to make sense of contradictory sources in tracing the route, has a touch of desperation in it; and the self that Thomas meets on the road has lost his bearings. These two men, the one who set out from Odsey and will arrive in Edlesborough, the other who does not know where he has come from or where he is going, alternate or coexist in various guises in Thomas's work. The dislocated quality of much of his prose is largely accounted for by this split, and testifies to the acuteness with which he felt it. The broken-backed chapter in *The Icknield Way* is one instance. Thomas's poetry is a last resort. There, with a subtle mixture of realist and symbolist elements which roughly corresponds to the division within himself — he is both at home and in exile, the world is both familiar and strange — he finds a more adequate way of representing the tensions under which he lived and the moments of resolution which made his life bearable.

Thomas denigrates himself, though perhaps with some pride, when he calls himself "a lean indefinite man". But if the phrase, with its touch of paradox (do the two adjectives compliment o contradict each other?), is applied to his poems, it becomes the expression of an aesthetic, exactly describing their qualities of language as well as the kinds of experience to which they respond. Thomas is close in some respects to the French Symbolists, whom he knew through Arthur Symons's critical writing and his own study of Maeterlinck. The "living and social words" which he aimed at in his struggle to shed the mannerism which, he complained, came naturally to him, were his own way of obeying Verlaine's command in the poem, 'Art Poétique', to "take eloquence and wring its neck". Verlaine's declaration in the same poem, that "there is nothing more precious than the grey song where the Undecided is joined to the Precise" (Anthony Hartley's translation) recalls the atmosphere of several of Thomas's poems, 'Old Man' for example. Thomas is also affected, less deeply but for similar reasons, by Imagist practice, which perhaps helped him to carry into verse the sharp observation of nature and country life which had previously found its place in the prose essay in the work of Richard Jefferies and W.H. Hudson and then in his own. Thomas the critic hovers between sympathy and hostility to the Symbolists and Imagists. But when he begins to write poetry himself their example is in his mind. His own intense technical preoccupation, arising from his need for poetic concentration, makes him sympathetic to theirs. It would have been against his nature — he had no taste for literary platforms — to write an equivalent of Verlaine's poem. But the imagery of Thomas's poetry constitutes a covert *ars poetica*. In particular he is drawn to artefacts which have lost their new-made look and taken on the appearance of natural objects, a barn with grass on the roof, old birds' nests, an abandoned chalk pit. The qualities of indistinctness, suggestiveness and secrecy which he finds in these are close to those cultivated by Symbolist poetry. The beautifully turned poem, 'Tall Nettles' exemplifies Thomas's method — if that is not too deliberate a word. Dust covers the nettles, and the nettles cover an accretion of old implements, "the rusty harrow, the plough...the roller made of stone:/ Only the elm butt tops the nettles now". These things, awkward to get rid of and left to lie in the corner of the farmyard, represent the residue at the bottom of the mind — "all that survives of thought and feeling", as Thomas phrased it when writing about Clare — which he believed to be the essential stuff of poetry.

The technical achievement of Thomas's poetry is usually considered to lie in its closeness to the idiom and rhythms of common speech. But Thomas's sense of the world must have faced him with at least as great a difficulty. "I should prefer the truth/ Or nothing", one of the speakers in 'The Chalk Pit' concludes. (Thomas's waywardness was the other face of a nature that was extreme and uncompromising.) But "the truth" and "nothing" are indescribable, however poetry tries to approach them, and Thomas is left with no other fixed points of belief within which to locate what he has to say. Robert Frost used to tease Thomas for not being able to make up his mind what direction to take when they went for walks together. 'The Road Not Taken' is the famous result. Frost trusts to impulse and chance. For Thomas choices are equally unconsidered; but that they do not present themselves as in Frost's poem is clear from the companion piece in his own work, 'The Signpost'. There he is left "Wondering where he shall journey, O where?", and still waiting for a fateful indication. Thomas believed that decisions, if they meant anything at all, were already made by the time they presented themselves at a conscious level. In his poetry too he stands out for his scrupulous inability to take paths which were not right for him or to conceal uncertainty. He returns constantly, for example, to his philosopher's puzzle, entangling himself almost as a habit of style in the question, Am I melancholy or happy? – only to find in poem after poem that these opposites merge into one another and become names for the same state. Like Frost, Thomas writes out of an overpowering sense of ignorance. Both men feel themselves to be face to face with an immense and uncontrollable darkness about which nothing can be understood. This shared sense may have been at the heart of their "friendship at first sight"; though Frost was a survivor and tends to fight the darkness, while Thomas tends to welcome it. Thomas's poems, with their sharp detail and their exact delineations of uncertainty, are small patches of clarity which blur off at the edges and cannot be fitted to any larger meaning. The theme of not being able to think, of not understanding, is a common one in his work. It is perhaps connected with the strong Puritan element in his nature, implanted by a Nonconformist upbringing. His remark in the last pages of his war diary, "I never understood quite what was meant by God", is close to William Cowper's "God moves in a mysterious way"; and his sense of mystery was intensified by the inexplicable visitations of depressive illness. Again, of patriotism he writes that it often comes down in the end to "I do not understand. I love", as if love, too, precluded understanding. Behind Thomas's partial attachment to Symbolist and Imagist methods lies a Puritan passion for reading the particulars of the world as signs. Thomas, as he looks about himself on the road, often reminds us of John Bunyan; but he is a pilgrim without religious belief and has no Celestial City to journey towards.

II

These remarks on Thomas's own nature and the nature of his poetry are a necessary preliminary to discovering something of what England means to him. If the 'nothing' in his poetry (it is one of his commonest words) is deathbound, standing for the depressive mood in which at best he did not care whether he lived or died, the 'truth' is summed up by him in the word 'England'. "She is all we know and live by", he declares, and that "She" is emphatic, recalling Thomas's remark in his essay, 'This England': "The old phrases come back alive in wartime. I have heard a farmer's wife refer to England as She". Thomas does not write well when he writes explicitly about England, and this profession of faith — that is what it is — occurs in the least successful of his poems, 'This is no case of petty right or wrong', in which he sets out his attitude to the war. Thomas begins by putting aside any distinction between right and wrong, and adds "But I have not to choose...between justice and injustice". He also dismisses what history might have to teach him. "Little I know or care if, being dull,/ I shall miss something that historians/ Can rake out of the ashes". For dispassionate moral and historical assessment he substitutes instinct and emotion. By the end of the poem his attitude is indistinguishable from that of the "fat patriot" whom he despises, and since argument has been disowned his own arguments have an air of special pleading. Thomas wrote 'This is no case of petty right or wrong' after a violent argument with his father about the war. His exasperated tone can be partly blamed on that; he is asserting himself against one fat patriot especially, and the poem is an episode in a much longer quarrel. It is doubtful if Thomas himself would have published it. He hated jingoism and was at pains to mark off from it his own love of country. He writes approvingly of the old soldier's attitude in 'It's a Long, Long Way', "His was a very little England. If England was against Germany, the parish was against England, Germany and all the world". Thomas is for the parish; his patriotism is local and particular in origin. Yet, speaking hastily, he betrays a habit of mind which surfaces at several points in his poetry and is implicit in much of the rest. Our attitude to this habit of mind will have a part in determining what Thomas's poetry means to us; the ways in which it speaks for us or does not.

Thomas shows little sense of the common tragedy in which Europe was caught by the war. It is hard to clear one's mind of the suspicion that his "English words" may be meant only for the English. The limit of his sympathy appears by contrast with Hardy's reaction. Hardy remarks in his sonnet, 'The Pity of It', on the similarities between the German language and the dialect "by-talk" which he hears as he walks "in loamy Wessex lanes". After the poem's publication Hardy commented in a letter, "People are in strangely irritable mood, I fancy. I said very harmlessly that the Germans were a 'kin folk, kin tongued' (which is indisputable) and letters attacking me appeared". When Hardy claims to be harmless it is as well to watch out. A reader of 'The Pity of It' might naturally have taken "gangs whose glory threats and slaughters are" to mean Germans only, but Hardy does not say so; and the poem concludes with a curse upon those responsible for the war, "whosoever they be". A similar reservation shadows the song, 'Men Who March Away':

> Is it a purblind prank, O think you,
>   Friend with the musing eye,
>   Who watch us stepping by
>   With doubt and dolorous sigh?
> Can much pondering so hoodwink you!

Again Hardy commented in a letter, "You may have suspected the 'Friend with the musing eye' to be the author himself". Hardy knew that the war meant the end of ameliorist Victorian hopes; his mind ran on what the cost would be in futile human suffering. Here he responds not with "faith and fire" but with "doubt and dolorous sigh", and with the ironic suggestion that it is the soldiers represented as singing the song who are hoodwinked. Understanding, for Hardy, means holding out against the blindness of things as clearsightedly as possible. The passage from Job which he chose to stand at the head of his *Collected Poems* (now given its place in Samuel Hynes's fine recent edition, which also draws attention to the passages from letters quoted above) reads, "That which I have seen I will declare". Hardy's moments of vision are moments of understanding. He does not wilfully disregard philosophers and historians but learns from them. Even at his most wooden or melodramatic he writes in the belief that art must consciously confront the great subjects, and this makes his Wessex a wider place than Thomas's England. For Thomas, sight is simply the physical sense, and understanding is not to be won by the conscious mind.

The doctrinaire tone of 'This is no case of petty right or wrong' reappears, though more mutedly, in 'The Manor Farm' and 'Haymaking', the two poems of his own which Thomas included in his anthology, *This England.* Thomas is not unthinking when in the last line of 'The Manor Farm', he speaks of "Merry" England. He does not mean that everything was well in the old days. He is, rather, admiring the ability to live in the present moment, without looking before and after, which "merry" indicates. To a man of his fretful temperament, an ingenuous cheerfulness and capacity for enjoyment were especially attractive qualities. But the conventional echoes in the phrase are also there and overwhelm the expression of need. A similar moment occurs toward the end of 'Haymaking'. Thomas believes that the scene described there, ideal in its freshness, will continue to recur, just as he believes that England will arise, magically rejuvenated, from the "witches' cauldron" of war, or that Lob, in the poem of that name, will continue to reappear in Wiltshire lanes (so that it does not much matter how often he is killed or in what cause). It would be easy to retort that history disproves Thomas, but his meaning is not so easily circumscribed. His feeling for the scene has a legendary dimension like that which Pasolini suggests in *Lettere Luterane*, though Pasolini is lamenting the end which Thomas does not foresee:

> For me the countryside meant a continuity, assured and unchanging, a reaching back of the human world to its origins; every gesture, every word became significant and took on an almost ritual quality.

Such scenes as that in 'Haymaking' give Thomas an inkling of something irreducible which he feels to be beyond the reach of historical or social change. But, as Raymond Williams has observed, the timelessness of the scene is too comfortably assumed, and the edge is taken off Thomas's belief.

Introducing *This England*, Thomas writes, "I wished to make a book as full of English character and country as an egg is of meat". Here and elsewhere in Thomas's writing this quality of Englishness is supposed to be self-evident, and almost no consideration is given to what it means. Why, for example, should 'When icicles hang by the wall', which Thomas gives as his instance of a "most English poem", be so, any more than another poem in the language? Thomas labours the Englishness without examining it, and the effect is to cloud natural affection and pride with an air of self-congratulation. First there is an implicit suggestion that what must be praised for being English cannot simply be praised for being good, and that one must be of the right descent to appreciate it properly. Second, what is claimed as English is made to serve an unadmittedly partial view of the tradition and is consequently distorted. Thomas's view of England is thoroughly stay-at-home. The England of travellers and translators, the country traditionally open to refugees, the home loved as a place to come back to rather than as a place never to leave; this England has little place in Thomas's poetry. "She could do no more with Samarcand", he writes in the poem to his youngest daughter. As Edna Longley points out, he has probably been put in mind of Samarkand by Flecker's poem. Flecker is not so good a poet as Thomas, but he stands for an admirable openness to other cultures. Thomas's poems contain only one traveller's tale — the startling simile in 'Swedes' where the newly-unroofed swede pile — "the white and gold and purple of curled fronds" — is contrasted with the dead splendours of archaeological discovery:

> It is a sight more tender-gorgeous...
> Than when, in the Valley of the Tombs of Kings,
> A boy crawls down into a Pharaoh's tomb
> And, first of Christian men, beholds the mummy...

The simile is almost beautiful. But beneath it lies Thomas's dislike of any organised system of knowledge. The archaeologist joins the historian and the philosopher as a figure for whom he has no use. The disdain is emphasised by what is perhaps a conscious error; for the boy, presumably an Egyptian, who crawls down into the tomb would almost certainly be a Muslim. Thomas is writing as nearly as possible in language which would be recognised by the labourers who unroofed the swede pile, and "first of Christian men" is the phrase which English naturally produces. But in the poem the phrase becomes a stumbling-block. Thomas's sense of English tradition is weighed against the intellectual and the cosmopolitan. He tends to smooth out what is partisan and argumentative in the matter of writers with whom he has a sympathy (though he may appreciate the manner). Clare and Cobbett were angry men, for good reasons, but the tone of 'Haymaking', in which their names occur, is one of sheer contentment. The names form part of a list and are hardly distinguished from one another; it is enough that they are "pure English" (as Thomas says elsewhere, in a foolish rhapsody on Cobbett's name). So with the list of battles in 'Lob'. Lob "was seen dying at Waterloo,/ Hastings, Agincourt, and Sedgmoor, too". But Sedgmoor was a battle in a civil war. Was Lob fighting for James or for Monmouth? If he was among those sentenced by Judge Jeffreys, was he perhaps also among the executioners? These episodes merge together, until the view of English history resembles that made fun of in *1066 and All That*. 'Lob' was a favourite poem of Thomas's, but what is real in it, the ghostly presence which puts on flesh to "keep clear old paths that no one uses", is overlaid by a mélange of picturesque country lore and speech which is little better than folksy, though it may be entertaining.

Thomas dwells on his lack of concern for history in *The South Country*.

> The truth is that though the past allures me... I have no historic sense and no curiosity. I have read a great deal of history...but I have forgotten it all, or it has got into my blood and is present in me in a form which defies evocation or analysis. But as far as I can tell I am pure of history.

Yet the conclusion that he is interested in the legend rather than the history of England must be qualified. First Thomas believes that it is by the legend that men are moved and there that events have their origin. In his England the heraldic beasts of his poetry come into their own, the badger in 'The Combe', the "great dragon" in 'Tears', the two cocks "Each facing each as in a coat of arms" in 'Cock-Crow'. It is a place of dreams, ghosts and signs, and these must be believed in if they are to be known. Dispassionate history may by comparison give only the illusion of understanding. A second qualification is that Thomas's sense of the past covers too great a time-span for history. "Time swims before me, making as a day/ A thousand years..." he writes in 'February Afternoon' (while making an observation about the way birds continuously settle forward of each other to feed that "last are first again", which as it happens has an exact parallel in the *Iliad*). The first chapter of *The Icknield Way* contains a powerful imaginative evocation of the life of men on the Downs in prehistoric times, which grows out of his thoughts on the relation of road to landscape. Thirdly, Thomas is before his time in requiring a history more concerned with locality and the anonymous dailiness of life. Above all, there is Thomas's acute sense of the effect of war, in numberless small shifts, upon the life and landscape of the country. The situation described in 'As the team's head brass' provides the outstanding example: the labourer who has been killed at the front; the felled elm he might have helped to shift; Thomas sitting in the elm's crest, talking to the ploughman; the existence of the poem itself. In Thomas's poetry the war is at the centre of a web of circumstance which touches on his surroundings at every point, just as it touches on his own mind as he remembers and observes.

Thomas's claim that he has no historic sense is not so absolute as it sounds. He means rather that his mind cannot grasp anything which does not touch on him directly. Knowledge for him is a matter of his own bodily experience. If that is what it must be for everyone at root, the difference is that Thomas will not allow it to be more than that. He cannot know anything at a remove and he does not believe in trying to get outside what he knows in order to have a view of it. "Everything/ To faintness like those rumours fades", he writes of his reflections about the war, on his walks with Frost; "our eyes/ Could as well imagine the Crusades/ Or Caesar's battles"; and in a letter to Frost about the possibility of his being sent to France, "I should like to see what it is like over there". Thomas has a strong feeling for the natural economy of memory. Old impressions must be allowed to die if they are to be succeeded by new, or if any selection among them is to be made. The historic sense, consciously exercised, can only interfere with the process. Physical sensation cannot be retained by the memory; it changes to something else (like the shrivelled corpse of the stoat which the gamekeeper in 'Under the Wood' has fixed to the shed wall); to be recollected it must be repeated. "The Past is a strange land", Thomas writes in 'Parting', and "The perished self...lacks all blood and nerve and wit". He used to curse himself for the habit of keeping notebooks, and his poems are as much concerned with forgetting as with remembering. His feeling for the process is at its clearest in 'The Word'.

> There are so many things I have forgot,
> That once were much to me, or that were not,
> All lost...

Among the "lesser things" which he remembers (prompted by a sensation, "the elder scent/ That is like food", "the wild rose scent that is like memory") is "an empty thingless name", "a pure thrush word", "cried out to me/ From somewhere in the bushes". History, for Thomas, can reduce itself to "a pure thrush word", instinctive and inarticulate.

Because Thomas is an artist and knows what he wants when he finds it, his sense of tradition is, at heart, as sound as the best of his poems. In particular he takes a convention of country writing, mostly in prose, which runs from Izaac Walton and Gilbert White to Richard Jefferies and W.H. Hudson, and transforms it. His poetry is like the waist of an hour-glass through which this tradition passes. Fined down, it becomes available to the poetry of this century, on which it has had a great though mostly hidden effect. Eliot writes of tradition," It cannot be inherited, and if you want it you must obtain it by great labour". Thomas takes the opposite view. Though it is difficult to imagine a man working harder, tradition remains for him an inherited instinct, and he interprets the rules that govern the inheritance rather narrowly. His distrust of conscious discrimination allows him to confuse the genuine tradition which he worked to find for himself with that baggy and unexamined package, the 'national heritage'. "We have each of us some of the blood and spirit of Sir Thomas More, and Sir Philip Sidney and the man who wrote *Tom Jones*, and Horatio Nelson, and the man who wrote *Love in the Valley*", Mr. Stodham declares in *The Happy-Go-Lucky Morgans*. "They are England: we are England. Deny England, and we deny them and ourselves". No picking and choosing is allowed, and so much the worse if we happen to dislike Fielding or Meredith. The chapter is headed 'Mr. Stodham Speaks for England — Fog Supervenes'. Mr. Stodham is being guyed by Thomas, but affectionately and with approval. In him Thomas is representing his own notion of England in all its proudly deliberate incoherence. A possible implication of this view is spelt out later in the novel when the Morgan household receives a visit from a bailiff, a caricatured figure of whom Thomas writes, "most of his face was nose". After the visit, the boy Philip is indignant:

> Philip, armed with a long-handled mallet, had constituted himself the English host on the hill brow, battering the Normans downhill with yells of 'Out, out,' and 'God Almighty,' and also 'Out Jew.' For his enemy was William of Normandy and the Jew bailiff in one. With growls of 'Out, out' through foaming set lips, he swung the mallet repeatedly, broke a Windsor chair all to pieces, and made the past live again.

Philip is perhaps fifteen years old; he too is being guyed, and this is a novel published in 1913. Thomas's usually gentle tone and his sense of decency help to protect him from facile xenophobia. But the logic of his position tends to make him the ally rather than the opponent of popular prejudice.

> But wiser is the man who laughs also,
> Or holds his laughter, when the foolish do.

The implication remains.

Thomas can be considered, in David Wright's words, as last of the line of English poets who...are...recorders and elegisers of "the slow destruction of rural England and its culture". But unlike his predecessors, he records passively and is unable to protest; not against the destruction of the culture nor against the mass slaughter of the men who embodied the culture. "Good-night. You keep straight on", he says to the labourer asking him directions in 'Man and Dog', and watches him disappear "in the twilight of the wood". The clods which he sees "crumble and topple over" in 'As the team's head brass' are also a human clay, "la terre charnelle" of Péguy. In 'It's a Long, Long Way', Thomas records the following snippet of conversation: " 'I wouldn't enlist for anything,' said a man with his cheese waiting on his knife-tip, 'not unless I was made. I would if it was a fair war. But it's not, it's murder' ". There's something dishonest about that detail of the cheese on the knife-tip. The protest should have an answer; but Thomas plays the reporter, while making the man appear slightly ridiculous. As we read the almost jaunty conversations about the war in Thomas's poetry, we reflect that it is usual now in English villages for the war memorial to contain more names than one sees people in the streets. Thomas seems to pick up and express a general will to die, of a kind which appears to lay hold of nations at times, gripping England in the years of the war as it has, for example, gripped contemporary Iran. It is impossible to work on the land or to spend much time walking over it without being conscious of its ghosts; the feet that made the roads, the hands that built the walls, above all the people who died to win the ground or to defend it. But Thomas's poetry speaks for an England that has been claimed by its ghosts, where it is time to find a way of joining them.

> Now all roads lead to France
> And heavy is the tread
> Of the living; but the dead
> Returning lightly dance...

England serves at first as a shield with which Thomas defends himself against his suicidal impulse. In Mr. Stodham's words:

> Deny England...and...you may have to deny your own self, and treat it as nothing, a mere conventional boundary, an artifice, by which you are separated from the universe and its creator. To unite yourself with the universe and the creator, you may be tempted to destroy that boundary of your own body and brain, and die.

With the war, Thomas's own private neurosis falls away in the general recognition of an extreme situation. But the shield has ceased to be a protection; it becomes a way of letting himself through to death. It turns out that the "truth" and the "nothing" in Thomas's work lead in one direction. Like happiness and melancholy, they become indistinguishable in the end.

III

"We are limited creatures", Thomas has Mr. Stodham say. The strength of Thomas's poetry, both technically and in its subject matter, is that he will not go beyond what he knows. He will take a matter only so far as he is sure of it and then he will leave it, as in those twin poems 'The Path' and 'The Lane'. The track suddenly fails; we are mysteriously glad and satisfied to have followed it, though not wiser in any way that we can explain. Thomas is characteristically at his best at his most inconsequential, though he also has an epigrammatic gift, and achieves in one poem, 'A Private', the perfection of a Greek anthology epitaph (in this it resembles Eliot's epigram on Phlebas the Phoenician, which also has as its occasion, though not overtly, a death in war). Thomas was a poor and busy man all his life. He hardly possessed the money or opportunity to leave England, had he wanted to (though he once managed a few days in Paris). What he knows and loves is inevitably English. The recurring experience of freshness and sweetness in the natural scene, which he also finds in some English writers, is certainly genuine. There is also the discovery of a melancholy which wants nothing more than to disappear into the landscape. And beneath, unintegrated, there runs a furious energy. We recognise this combination in England today, though the sweetness becomes harder to find. But Thomas breaks his own rule. He goes beyond the particularities of his experience and makes England into a substitute for a religious belief, a way of compensating for that absence of larger meaning in which his poems hang suspended. He even appears to believe that the war may be a death from which England will rise again, purified and revealed in her true nature. Thomas is the wayward pilgrim to whom England gives a faith and a direction. This means that England and English tradition, as he conceived them, are put beyond critical examination, and that his own intelligence is partially disabled.

Another consequence of the insistence on limits is that Thomas writes about England as if it were a civilisation entire in itself, as for example the Greeks marked themselves off from non-Greeks — though this was a matter of way of life rather than of race. He never makes it clear why the "system of vast circumferences circling round the minute neighbouring points of home", which he believes England to be, should stop with its shores and not continue outward. His England is always in opposition. It is the place that is not France, not Germany. English culture can be falsified and depleted by being cut off in this way. Thomas acknowledges that it is a part of a larger culture in some of his criticism, and tacitly in his debt to Symbolism. It is striking that the advice which turned Thomas towards writing poetry came from his only close non-English friend, Robert Frost. But there is a vein of wilful insularity in his work which makes the cult that has grown up around him very suspect. He has become his admirers, with a vengeance. The sentimentality that attaches itself to him is exemplified by the inscription on the memorial stone at Steep, which begins, "This hillside is dedicated to the memory of Edward Thomas". Only a made thing can be dedicated. Dedicating a hillside is laughable, as well as presumptuous. The other side of this sentimentality, we may suspect, is spoken for by Philip's outburst in *The Happy-Go-Lucky Morgans.* Readers whose loyalties are not so easily bounded by the name of a country as Thomas assumes will inevitably have a reservation about his poetry. Usually it is no more than a shadow, but it can only be wished away if we take no notice of what he thinks, and it can harden into a problem of belief. Thomas would simply shrug his shoulders and say that we were always at liberty to "like a different tree". But in the England of the mid-eighties, where the "Sweet Stay-at-Home, sweet Well-content" of W.H. Davies's poem has turned sour and disgruntled, we need to quarrel with Thomas as well as to admire him.

SALLY ROBERTS JONES

Edward Thomas and Wales

Edward Thomas and Wales

At one time it was the custom to claim any writer with even the slightest connection with Wales as a Welsh writer, and the fledgeling Anglo-Welsh tradition acquired such figures as John Donne, George Meredith and Wilfred Owen. In some cases further investigation does suggest a genuine claim to a place in the succession, but far more often over-enthusiastic support of dubious candidates has led to a rejection of others with much more solid claims.

Edward Thomas saw himself as a Welshman — though one 'accidentally' born and brought up in the suburbs of London, and therefore not entirely typical. His friends also noted the Welsh connection, and yet one finds Walter De La Mare writing (in 1920), "When, indeed, Edward Thomas was killed in Flanders, a mirror of England was shattered of so pure and true a crystal that a clearer and tenderer reflection of it can be found no other where than in these poems."

Welsh critics, too, have tended to reject him as a writer of Welsh relevance. Alun John remarks, "No-one can dispute that Edward Thomas came of Welsh stock or that he had personal connections with Wales.... Some of the books and essays he wrote before 1914 carried many references to Wales and its people, its places and its scenery" — a nice example of damning with faint praise. Again, in the Edward Thomas centenary number of *Poetry Wales*, in 'Edward Thomas and Wales', we read "In 1889 in Clapham the Thomases found themselves living next door to a Welsh family.... Thomas seems to have become interested in them and their country." Partly, of course, this is due to the peculiarly Welsh habit of regarding every Welshman who sets foot east of Offa's Dyke (or even south of Aberystwyth) as a non-person, and partly due to the simplistic approach that sees Anglo-Welsh literature as a matter of Welsh settings and references. However, in Edward Thomas's case it is further complicated by the fact that we see him basically through the eyes of Helen, his wife, and his other English friends, which leads to a certain imbalance in most accounts of his life and work.

Since this imbalance begins with the poet's family background — "for there was Spanish blood, as well as Devonshire and Welsh in his veins" — perhaps it would be best to start with that family background and Thomas's own acquaintance with Wales. Philip Henry Thomas, the poet's father, was the grandson of Thomas Thomas of Cwmavon (Port Talbot); the Eastaway/Treharne connection came from this branch, and possibly Thomas Thomas married a Miss Eastaway since their children included Henry Eastaway Thomas (Philip Henry's father) and Caroline Eastaway Thomas. Henry Eastaway Thomas moved to Tredegar, where he worked as a fitter, and married Rachel Phillips of Abertillery (Edward Thomas's 'Swindon grandmother'). Perhaps one should note here that families like the Eastaways, Treharnes, Lovelucks and Heycocks, though bearing witness to the cross-channel trade between Wales and the West Country, have often been effectively Welsh for several centuries.

Edward Thomas's mother was born Mary Elizabeth Townsend, daughter of Edward Thomas Townsend of Newport in Gwent, and of Catherine Ann Marendaz of Margam, Port Talbot. Catherine Ann died young, twenty years before Edward Thomas himself was born, but her mother, the poet's great-grandmother, lived on until 1893 and may well have been the source of Thomas's knowledge of his 'Spanish sea captain' ancestor, David Emmanuel Marendaz Senior (her father-in-law), and of the captain's gold signet ring, eventually given to Helen Thomas. By family tradition Marendaz was Portuguese, and is said to have saved the life of T.M. Talbot of Margam when the latter was on a Mediterranean yachting trip. Talbot brought Marendaz back with him, lent him money, and made a farm available for him at a peppercorn rent. It is possible that this patronage had a more than romantic significance for Edward Thomas; the Talbots were in the habit of sponsoring promising young artists and musicians, and could well have had something to do with Thomas's otherwise very unlikely sojourn at St. Paul's School, perhaps by helping with his school fees, and even at Oxford. (The evidence is tenuous, but relevant.)

From this it becomes clear that, though they lived in London, the Thomas family were essentially Welsh — even Welsh-speaking as far as Mr. Thomas was concerned; several of the maids-of-all work who helped Mrs. Thomas came from Wales, and though the younger generation learnt only a smattering of Welsh words (and it is unlikely that Mrs. Thomas spoke it) they must all have been used to the sound of the language around them. More relevantly, perhaps, the ideas that formed Philip Henry Thomas's opinions and behaviour, and which he passed on to his sons, to accept or react against, were formed by a Welsh upbringing, not by the conventions of English suburbia. The long family holidays at Swindon were also spent in a 'Welsh' environment, as Edward Thomas makes clear in *The Childhood of Edward Thomas*.

As for more direct contact with Wales, Thomas visited south Wales twice as a child, both times taken by his mother; on the first occasion, when he was about five, they visited Caerleon, Swansea and Newport, and the second time they went to Abertillery. Both visits made a considerable impression on him. His adult experience of Wales began in 1896 when he was eighteen; he spent a large part of the summer and autumn in Gower and Pontardulais, where he met the Welsh-language poet Gwili who became a life-long friend. These visits were a family affair; Thomas's younger brothers were also there, and there was talk of sending them to Watkyn Wyn's Academy at Ammanford (an odd, and very Welsh, contrast to St.Paul's School). From that point on he spent a significant period in Wales almost every year until he enlisted in the army in 1915. (There was apparently a break in 1901-3, when his own children were small and money was tight.)

On the other hand, this was in-depth experience of a comparatively small area; he knew Glamorgan, Carmarthenshire, Pembrokeshire and southern Cardiganshire in considerable detail, but not the romantic castles and mountains of north Wales that were so much better known outside Wales. Hence his difficulty when he was commissioned to write *Beautiful Wales*. He had already written *Oxford* for the same series (Black's Colour Book Series); he knew the university well enough to produce a book that could serve as a guide book as well as reflecting its author's own interests. Wales was another matter. To begin with, he was supposed to write a text to accompany the really important part of the book: seventy-four paintings by Robert Fowler. (The first edition includes a twelve-page article on the artist — but nothing, naturally, on the author; it is also so heavily interlined with illustrations that it is not easy to get at the text.) A.G.Bradley, who wrote a companion volume on the Wye, produced a simple guide, following the course of the river, but Bradley had walked or ridden from end to end of the country and knew it intimately. Edward Thomas had that sort of knowledge of his own corner of Wales, but unfortunately Robert Fowler's connections were with north Wales, as were most of his paintings.

Thomas could, of course, have written of his own region, but that option was not really open to him. London publishers tend to have their own image of Wales, and at that time romantic north Wales *was* that image (even the comparatively newly-created mining valleys were marginal then), and somehow Thomas had to find a compromise. This he did by omitting almost all place-names and generalising the descriptions, then including numerous character sketches of Welshmen — a minister, an inn-keeper, a bard (though his 'Poacher' smacks more of Wiltshire than Wales), and ending up with what purport to be descriptions of Wales through the months — it is not surprising to learn from Alun John that these "were culled almost entirely from the notes he had previously made of the countryside of England." Altogether, *Beautiful Wales* is probably the least Welsh of his books in any meaningful sense. (Though the habit of not-naming and the prose-poetic vagueness seem to have had sufficient audience success for him to use them again, in *The South Country*, for example.)

Something of what Thomas's dedicated research *could* have achieved with *Beautiful Wales* can be seen from his essays on 'Swansea Village' and 'Glamorgan' in *The Last Sheaf*. They stand at the other end of his career, of course, when he had at last achieved "the simple prose which he finally decided was the best of all... 'as near akin as possible to the talk of a Surrey peasant' ", but they have all the vigour and clarity that the earlier book lacked.

> But this I cannot understand: that some people should be — and some are — indifferent to Swansea. Year after year I go there (I do not mean to the Mumbles, but to the town, and nothing but the town), and walking up and down it and round about, inhaling sea air and mountain air, or the smells from copper works, cobalt works, manure works, and fried-fish shops; year after year I have felt that only friends could bring me again to Swansea.

In the Swansea essay, too, he expresses something which is typical of Anglo-Welsh writing — that interplay between the industrial and rural landscape which means that such writing almost never becomes completely urbanised:

> ...this chapel is at the foot of a rough quarried slope sprinkled thinly and anyhow with white and whitish cottages among rushes and tufted grass, which is a scene of an almost moorland sweetness for those living in the new-old streets of eternal smoke under the mountain opposite, barren and black.

It is clear that the visible evidence of Thomas's connection with Wales is only a small part of what existed. Welsh references crop up everywhere; in *The Country* he writes: "For Nature includes Fleet Street as well as the Milky Way, Whitechapel as well as the valley of the Towey or the valley of the Wylye...or we are proud that the rain on the windy bus-top has kissed us exactly as on Old Winchester Hill or Sir John's Hill at Laugharne and has brought them to mind." Later he quotes at length from a Welsh poem in translation, but there are no equivalent precise English references in the book. Elsewhere he speaks of visiting Swansea "as often as four times in a year", which suggests that he made many shorter, unrecorded visits to the area.

To Edward Thomas, of course, there was no automatic conflict between love for his adopted country, England, and his ancestral home, Wales, as there has been for some later, more nationalistically-inclined Anglo-Welsh poets. (Though 'his' England was only a small known part of that country — the quotation from *The Country* draws its limits neatly — Whitechapel, Winchester, the valley of the Wylye.) And his Welsh background — the assumptions that his parents and grandparents had passed on to him — gave him the chance of entry to areas of English country life which his English contemporaries would not have appreciated. It was this, rather than a difference in hobbies, which led to the often-quoted exchange (from *The Childhood of Edward Thomas*) at St. Paul's School: " 'What are you reading,

Thomas?' asked one of the boys who already wore a scholar's gown. '*The Gamekeeper at Home*' said I. 'The gamekeeper's place is in the woods,' said he. And I kept silence, not venturing to remark that the woods were his home." 'Dad' Uzzell, Thomas's Wiltshire friend and mentor, would have been quite inaccessible to the young gentleman in the scholar's gown, even had he felt the countryman worthy of his attention.

Through his friend Gwili, Thomas had access to Welsh literature and history in its fullness (and not merely to the fashionable Celticism of the turn of the century), but it would probably be pointless to look for the use of technical innovations based on Welsh forms in his poems. The Welsh strict metres suit the Welsh language, but it takes a very exceptional writer, such as John Ormond, to transfer them into English without producing something totally artificial, and Edward Thomas was working towards simplicity and clarity of expression, not things that Anglicised cynghanedd was likely to produce. Wales had far more to offer in terms of subject material, and he was able to make use of this to fill out his commissioned work as well as in the uncommissioned essays that he wrote for himself. As for his poems, these are rarely specific; there *are* odd references to Wales or poems about subjects we know to be Welsh — 'The Mountain Chapel', 'Roads', 'The Ash Grove' — and the child in 'The Child on the Cliff' seems to be sitting on a Gower cliff, looking out over the drowned Coed Arian to the Devon coast. But this is no more relevant than the fact that the forest of 'The Green Roads' is Epping Forest, one of the main bridle paths of which is the Green Ride. It adds a minor pleasure for anyone who knows the Forest, but the landscape Thomas wrote of, though it draws on the elements of what he knew, is a country of the mind.

The 'Welshness' of Thomas's poetry, like that of his friend W.H. Davies, lies in something less obvious than geographical references or technical innovations, and it is also one reason why both poets have been associated, somewhat unhelpfully, with the Georgians (whom, of course, they did know well). The desire to return to simplicity and directness of language is an old theme in English literature — Wordsworth and the *Lyrical Ballads* are the best example — but basically the majority of English writers are middle-class, writing for the middle-classes. (This appears so self-evident that in one feminist anthology the compiler wrote 'the writing — i.e. the middle — classes'.) When W.H. Davies began to write, he started from a background and with an assumed audience which was very different, and though his first readers selected the pastoral image of 'What is this life...', which suited their own bias towards nature poetry, the latest edition of Davies's verse, (Oxford University Press, 1985), shows a much wider range of experience and sympathy. Edward Thomas's earliest influences, however, were late Victorian, English and literary-academic, and not surprisingly they formed the style in which he began to write — inflated and hazily romantic. (One has to remember, too, that much of his prose was a commercial product, on themes and in modes that were to a large extent dictated to him.) From this he moved, over the years, to a style that was not so much simple as universal, available to all potential readers, not just to 'country weekenders'. To quote Walter De La Mare: "There is nothing precious, elaborate, brilliant, esoteric, obscure in his work... [The poetry] ennobles by simplification.... These poems...tell...of Thomas's daily, and, one might say, common experience."

The difference of approach is less easy to demonstrate than it is for W.H. Davies, but it emerges, for instance, if one compares Thomas's easy acceptance of birds' nesting on the grand scale, or his poem 'The Gallows', with the popular Georgian attitude of Hodgson's: " 'Twould ring the bells of Heaven/ The wildest peal for years,/ If Parson lost his senses/ And people came to theirs..."; the pathetic fallacy rarely, if ever, appears in his work.

This accessibility in this form is a very Welsh characteristic (and it is one reason, I suspect, why Anglo-Welsh writers so often seem to be working below their ability); the main tradition develops not through the scholar in his study or the University wit, but through the bard or story-teller, in king's hall or kitchen, who must be accessible to the widest possible audience in order to survive. (The importance of story-telling and reading aloud in the Thomas household is very clear from *The Childhood of Edward Thomas*; it bore fruit eventually in the episodic framework of *The Happy-Go-Lucky Morgans*.) In fact, the simple story (or poem) becomes a vessel which holds much more than its obvious meaning — like the very best children's literature, which must please both child and parent. (In this context one might also comment on Thomas's frequent use of character sketches; full scale biography is not an Anglo-Welsh speciality, but portraits definitely are, as a glance at any anthology will show.)

Edward Thomas had one other legacy from his Welsh ancestry: the sense of isolation, social and intellectual, which had such an effect on the course of his life. The social isolation was probably most evident when he was at St. Paul's School: "I felt unimportant, isolated, out of place, and only not despised because I was utterly unnoticed.". However successful Mr. Thomas may have been eventually, neither he nor his resources were equal at that point to the world in which he wished to place his son. Later, accepted socially (as Anglo-Welsh writers tend to be in England, even when their background is very different to that of the cultural circles in which they move — c.f. W.H. Davies and Dylan Thomas), the isolation became an intellectual difference. Thomas himself describes it in his incomplete fragment 'Fiction': "For the people were no longer a negatively friendly element which the individual slid into and out of.... Perhaps I discerned something they had in common, but what I saw chiefly was that they were different from me." A little further on he describes how he walked into Salisbury one evening "feeling like a pirate or Border robber descending upon capon-fed middlemen, moneylenders, retired or expecting to retire." It is a sensation more frequently documented in conversation than in print, but one that seems valid for many Anglo-Welsh writers who find themselves in England. (It lies behind some of John Tripp's London poems.)

Although he tried to spend more time in the country (as in 1908 with the abortive post on the Royal Commission on Ancient Monuments), there was no practical possibility of Thomas's 'returning' to Wales as a later generation of Anglo-Welsh writers could. He earned his living as a freelance writer, and because of this even his life in Kent and Hampshire was disturbed by the need for fairly frequent visits to London. Wales became his unattainable 'other country' — at least as far as that had an earthly being. But within that context Wales appears everywhere throughout his work — and perhaps he loved England all the more, and appreciated its richness *because* of that other attachment. As Mr. Stodham says in *The Happy-Go-Lucky Morgans*: "Do you love the Wilderness? Do you love Wales? If you do, you love what I understand by 'England'. The more you love and know England, the more deeply you can love the Wilderness and Wales. I am sure of it...". Walter De La Mare spoke more truly than he probably knew when he described Edward Thomas as "a mirror of England" — a mirror that reflects, but is not, in the end, the thing it reflects.

BIBLIOGRAPHY

Edward Thomas: *Collected Poems* (Selwyn & Blount, 1920 & Faber, 1936). Introduction by Walter De La Mare.

Alun John: 'Edward Thomas: Anniversary Considerations'. In *Anglo-Welsh Review*, No.38, Winter 1967, pp.48-58.

'Edward Thomas and Wales'. In *Poetry Wales*, Vol.13, No.4, Spring 1978, pp.102-6. (Centenary Issue).

A. Leslie Evans: 'The Marendaz Family and the Poet, Edward Thomas'. In *Transactions of the Port Talbot Historical Society* Vol.1, No.3 (1967), pp.107-110.

Edward Thomas: *The Childhood of Edward Thomas* (Faber, 1938/83).

R. George Thomas: *Edward Thomas: a Portrait* (Oxford University Press 1985).

Edward Thomas: *Beautiful Wales* (A. & C. Black, 1905).

Roland Mathias: 'The South Country' (review). In *Anglo-Welsh Review*, No.81, 1985, pp.136-9.

Edward Thomas: *The Last Sheaf* (Jonathan Cape, 1928).

Edward Thomas: *The Country* (Batsford, 1913).

Edward Thomas: *Collected Poems* (O.U.P. 1981).

Edward Thomas: *The Happy-Go-Lucky Morgans* (Duckworth, 1913).

JEREMY HOOKER

From Graven Image to Speech: the Prose of Edward Thomas

From Graven Image to Speech: the Prose of Edward Thomas

There is nothing left for us to rest upon, nothing great, venerable, or mysterious, which can take us out of ourselves, and give us that more than human tranquillity now to be seen in a few old faces of a disappearing generation.[1]

(Edward Thomas, *The Country*)

Formerly, it was common for Edward Thomas's prose as a whole to be dismissed indiscriminately as hack work. Now, we are more in danger of overestimating the consistency of its development, and its continuity with the poetry. Edna Longley's fine anthology, *A language not to be betrayed* (1981), for example, represents Thomas mainly as a literary critic. He was the outstanding English critic of his generation. Moreover, he established in his criticism, at least as early as *Richard Jefferies* (1909), and with increasing confidence in his books on Maurice Maeterlinck and Walter Pater, published in 1911 and 1913 respectively, the principles of the poetry that he had still to write. Indeed, he not only established the principles, he wrote of language and style with the poet's authority. Yet he continued to write prose that was vitiated by original weaknesses.

In a relatively short writing life, Edward Thomas wrote more than thirty books, edited more than a dozen more, and produced a vast number of book reviews. He wrote in a variety of forms — description, diary, itinerary, biography, criticism, fiction, autobiography, prose poetry — and frequently mixed them. His books about nature and the country, in particular, mix description and observation with reverie, imaginative recreation, and lightly disguised spiritual autobiography. While this was permitted by this loosely defined kind of book, it is still remarkable how liberally Edward Thomas interpreted his commissions, especially in putting so much of himself into the landscapes. The restless, unsatisfactory experimental nature of much of the prose manifests acute formal problems. These relate intimately to problems with the self, for his prose is the record of his struggle to achieve an adequate means of self-expression. But he had first to know and believe in the self that he desired to express, and this meant, in terms which he used in *The Country* (1913), finding something larger than the self "to rest upon" (p.6).

Edward Thomas's first book, *The Woodland Life* (1897), consists of articles and a nature diary which he wrote while still in his teens. As he noted in his maturity, the young writer had "a grandiloquent turn".[2] He had, also, a gift of observation, a microscopic eye, and the ability to arrange his observations. Thus, he perceives a dead leaf:

> On the green mound lies a dead oak-leaf, sober brown and nothing more to the first glance. Through the winter it has lain there, while some of its fellows yet cling wizened and wan about the saplings. Its scalloped edge has kept intact in spite of wind and rain and frost. With the process of the months it has darkened and curled, till now it is a semi-cylinder of the hue of old leather; but underneath the plain brown surface shows a beautiful variety of shades — amber streaks, strange mottlings of chestnut, red and tawny, and, breaking through all, a bloom of faint gold. Each different tinge glows richly as the sunbeams light up the glossy curving surface. It is a last remnant of winter and of the bygone year, pillowed among the tender growths of early spring — sere brown set in the midst of youthful verdure. (p.9)

In the progressive revelation of what "the first glance" misses, this resembles the writing of Richard Jefferies, whose great influence on his life and work Edward Thomas acknowledged. Jefferies frequently begins with a small, easily overlooked detail of animate or inanimate nature, and magnifies it until its character, function, and place in the environment are revealed. In 'The Pageant of Summer', for example, he begins with green rushes. There is, however, a crucial difference between Jefferies's rushes and Thomas's dead leaf. For Jefferies reveals the life of the plant, whereas Thomas, in spite of making the dead leaf a symbol of winter among the signs of spring, sees it aesthetically, and makes a picture from its colours and sculptural shape. This is, in fact, close to the method of Walter Pater, which Thomas would describe later with devastating effect. In *The Woodland Life* the aesthetic mode of perception is dominant, but its tension with natural vision, which sees and depicts the life in things, is largely resolved by the joy of the young writer-cum-naturalist in exercising his gifts. The diary included in the book exhibits an art of naming, with a corresponding delight in the thing named, that is closer in fact to Thomas's poetry. First, though, he has to undertake a long struggle to relate aesthetic vision and natural vision, instead of obscuring and even betraying the latter with his word painting.

Recording his response to the nightingale's song in *The South Country* (1909), Edward Thomas says the notes, with their "inhumanity", convey "the mysterious sense...that earth is something more than a human estate". "Here for this hour we are remote from the parochialism of humanity. The bird has admitted a larger air. We breathe deeply of it and are made free citizens of eternity"(pp.35-36). "The larger air", for which Thomas often expresses desire, echoes the closing words of Jefferies's *The Amateur Poacher*, which for Thomas as a young man were "a gospel, an incantation"[3]: "Let us get out of these indoor narrow modern days, whose twelve hours somehow have become shortened, into the sunlight and the pure wind. A something that the ancients called divine can be found and felt there still". Freedom from "the parochialism of humanity" is a great theme, but Thomas is rarely able to pursue it with confidence for long. Thus, in *In Pursuit of Spring* (1914), he says Salisbury Plain "makes us feel the age of the earth, the greatness of Time, Space, and Nature; the littleness of man even in an aeroplane, the fact that the earth does not belong to man, but man to the earth". This is a feeling capable of generating awe, and in the writings of Richard Jefferies and W.H. Hudson, for example, it frequently does. But although Edward Thomas shares the feeling, his difference from them is marked by his self-conscious turning back upon himself: "And this feeling, or some variety of it, for most men is accompanied by melancholy, or is held to be the same thing. This is perhaps particularly so with townsmen, and above all with writers, because melancholy is the mood most easily given an appearance of profundity, and, therefore, most easily impressive" (p.150).

In *Richard Jefferies* Edward Thomas calls self-consciousness "perhaps, the most tragic condition of man's greatness". "If the sea-waves were to be self-conscious," he says, "they would cease to wash the shore; a self-conscious world would fester and stink in a month" (p.305). He was one who survived "the terror"; he even made a virtue of it in his poetry, but time and again in his prose, self-consciousness breaks in, interrupting its movement and concentration. It is at the roots of his problems as a prose-writer, and is a psychological dis-ease with social origins.

By the time he wrote his book on Walter Pater, Edward Thomas understood the problem in depth:

> men understand now the impossibility of speaking aloud all that is within them, and if they do not speak it, they cannot write as they speak. The most they can do is to write as they would speak in a less solitary world. A man cannot say all that is in his heart to a woman or another man. The waters are too deep between us. We have not the confidence in what is within us, nor in our voices. (p.208)

Inability to communicate is a consequence of isolation, which is the modern condition, dividing the individual both from others and from his own inner depths, so that he has confidence neither in himself nor in his voice. Edward Thomas's understanding of isolation inevitably owed much to his personal history. One of his many alter egos, the town-bred clerk escaping to the country, in *The South Country*, says: "I realize that I belong to the suburbs still". "As for myself," he continues, "I am world-conscious, and hence suffer unutterable loneliness" (p.89). Such figures at once reflect Thomas's situation and sentiments, and distance him self-critically from emotional extravagance. Born and brought up in the London suburbs, he early identified Wales, his parents' original country, as "my soul's native land".[4] Later, he found in southern England "a kind of home, as I think it is more than any other to those modern people who belong nowhere".[5] Ironically, but not surprisingly, some of his most effective prose, in *The Childhood of Edward Thomas* and *The Happy-Go-Lucky Morgans* (1913), explores the suburbs, while his descriptions of the country are frequently weakened by the escapism that arises from his lack of a necessary relation to it. For, as he says in *The Country*: "only a rarefied conscious appreciation is made possible by detachment and the severing of all bonds of necessity" (p.31). This is by no means the whole truth of his relation to nature and rural England, but the social and psychological forces isolating him were formidable. Moreover, they were fortified by his strongest, and otherwise opposing, literary influences: by the nature mysticism of *The Story of My Heart*, in which Jefferies, abstracted from the circumstances of his life and all relationships, stands "bare-headed before the sun, in the presence of the earth and air, in the presence of the immense forces of the universe", and by Pater's solipsism, in which experience "is ringed round for each one of us by that thick wall of personality through which no real voice has ever pierced on its way to us, or from us to that which we can only conjecture to be without", and every impression "is the impression of the individual in his isolation, each mind keeping as a solitary prisoner its own dream of a world".[6] In addition, Thomas's contempt for his readership, the "villa residents" discussed in *The Country*, exacerbated his lack of confidence and self-disgust, and increased his uncertainty of tone and focus. Self-consciousness made him his own severest critic, too. "I rarely see much in the country," he confesses in *The Heart of England* (1906); "I always carry out into the fields a vast baggage of prejudices from books and strong characters whom I have met". He proceeds to condemn in himself "the egoism of an imitative brain" (pp.133-134). Later, after he had begun to write poetry he spoke to Eleanor Farjeon of the "rhetoric and formality which left my prose so often with a dead rhythm only".[7] The curiously unmemorable quality of his prose especially at its 'finest' is due to its lack of a living rhythm. This in turn is due to the exclusively 'written' character which is a product of the isolated, self-conscious literary mind.

Edward Thomas's strongest description of the imagination occurs in Richard Jefferies:

> The clearness of the physical is allied to the penetration of the spiritual vision. For both are nourished to their perfect flowering by the habit of

> concentration. To see a thing as clearly as he saw the sun-painted yellow-hammer in Stewart's Mash is part of the office of the imagination. Imagination is no more than the making of graven images, whether of things on the earth or in the mind. To make them, clear concentrated sight and patient mind are the most necessary things after love; and these two are the children of love.
> (p.49)

Here, he is in process of making a distinction, but has not quite completed it. For clear seeing, attributed to Jefferies, is radically different from the "graven images" which Pater made from the life of things. In *Walter Pater* Thomas would describe him as "a spectator. His aim is to see; if he is to become something it is by seeing" (p.73). He would describe the style, "free from traces of experience" (p.109), in which Pater, in words that are "anything but living and social words" (p.213), turns life into art. Pater transforms "animate and inanimate things into words like graven images" (p.183). Clearly, that is not the kind of seeing or writing that Thomas admires in Jefferies.

Thomas continues his definition of imagination in *Richard Jefferies* by saying that those who have the rare "power of repeating these images by music or language or carved stone" are "aware that human life, nature, and art are every moment continuing and augmenting the Creation — making to-day the first day, and this field Eden, annihilating time" (p.49). He identifies imagination not with the historical present but with myth, his vision of Eden. But his idea of imagination also contains another meaning, fruitful with possibilities, although it too has a mythical dimension. Thomas mythologizes Jefferies, eloquently: "He...was the genius, the human expression, of this country, emerging from it, not to be detached from it any more than the curves of some statues from their maternal stone" (p.1). He sees Jefferies, however, not only as earth-born but as a man with something "to rest upon", a man with a people, who "came to express part of this silence of uncounted generations" (p.22). Thomas sees Jefferies's writing career much as we may now see his own: as a progressive self-revelation. By the time he writes *The Story of My Heart*, Jefferies is "the poet, the larger man who, though exquisitely sensitive, has no mere delicacy and rejected no part of life in man or nature, country or town" (p.180). He has "the clear vision that saw in all forms of life one commonwealth, one law, one beauty" (p.194). He is therefore, in spite of his loneliness, the opposite of the "isolated selfconsidering brain"[8], which Thomas, at his worst, felt himself to be, and his seeing has nothing in common with that of the spectator, who petrifies life in graven images. Thomas says of Jefferies's style that, "given an entirely suitable subject, he wrote with a natural fineness and richness and a carelessness, too, like the blackbird's singing" (p.179). It was in Jefferies, then, that Thomas first found his ideal of writing that is the natural speech of the whole man. Significantly, Jefferies dictated his last essays, and it is of these that Thomas says: "he has found himself; and now it is no longer the sportsman, or the naturalist, or the agriculturalist, or the colourist, or the mystic, that speaks, but a man who has played these parts and been worn and shaped by them, by work and pain" (p.313). Thomas found, in different degrees, the style that is the speech of "the poet, the larger man" in other writers whom he admired, in Cobbett and Hudson, for example, and, at a decisive moment, in the poetry of Robert Frost, whose *North of Boston* "speaks, and it is poetry".[9] It is what poetry finally released in Thomas himself but his prose almost always withheld.

Early in his writing career, Edward Thomas attempted to transcend the limitations of the aesthetic vision by peopling nature with mythological presences. In *Oxford* (1903), he claims to have "on several afternoons gone some way towards the beginning of a new mythology" (p.251). However, it is of Apollo and Diana that he thinks in the Oxfordshire countryside. In *Beautiful Wales* (1905), an old abbey provokes a characteristic reverie, in which he says that the reader too, if properly receptive, may seem there "to be on the edge of a new mythology and to taste the joy of the surmises of him who first saw Pan among the sedges or the olives" (pp.152-153). Only at the end did he cease entirely to superimpose the paraphernalia of classical mythology or the Celtic twilight on his prose descriptions of peopled, historical landscapes. It is not surprising, though, that a young writer should indulge in fancies and fantasies common to his literary period. What is harder to accept is that Edward Thomas's prose, early and late, is marked by the escapism, sentimentality, whimsy and general unreality for which Georgian poetry at its worst has been criticised. This is less surprising, however, if we reflect that the gap between poetry and experience, and the struggle of the best poets to close it, is the story of poetry in English in the opening decades of this century. In different ways, Edward Thomas in his poetry, and W.B. Yeats and Wilfred Owen, all closed the gap between poetry and experience, but by developing and deepening their romanticism, rather than by rejecting it. In Thomas's case, this may be illustrated by the following description of a house, from *The South Country*:

> The little old house rippled over by creeper was beautiful then — the lime tree and the creeper trembling in the gusty moonlight, and the windows and doorway hollow and dark and romantic as if a poet had made them to sting men's hearts with beauty and with regret. (p.67)

At first, it is hard to believe that any one who cherished such a sentimental notion of poetry could ever become a real poet. Yet important elements of this passage, the words "hollow and dark", the ideal of beauty, and the connection of beauty and regret, were springs of Edward Thomas's imagination, and appeared again, renewed, in the poetry. Renewed, but, I now think, more limited by their original source than is generally recognised.

We sentimentalize Edward Thomas by valuing him exclusively in terms of "a language not to be betrayed", instead of seeing him as a writer whose natural vision and speech, freed at last by his efforts from the prison of Romantic decadence, were not untouched by its shadow.

It is instructive to follow the last quotation with a passage from 'Hawthornden', in *Light and Twilight* (1911):

> It was literature, nevertheless, and the stage, that had given him the standard which he unconsciously applied to scenes in life which he thought should have been heroical, for example, and were not. Nor was he shaken from his dim-pinnacled citadel of unreality by his own experience of something near tragedy at home. His wife rushed at him one day, with stiff, drawn, red-spotted face and staring eyes, and a shrill voice he had never heard before, to tell him that one of the children was injured. He drew her head to his breast and kissed her hair, and felt at first a kind of shame, then an instinctive disgust at the stains and rude prints of her grief. (pp.121-122)

This both criticises the spectatorial, aesthetic attitude, and illustrates its capacity for cruelty. Hawthornden is one of Thomas's many partial self-portraits, and the passage reveals and analyses the detached, cold, even cruel vision that is a consequence of excessive romantic idealism. His detachment made him, at times, an acute psychological realist, and in *The Childhood of Edward Thomas*, in particular, he turns a clinical eye on himself as well as on other people. The result is sometimes rather disturbing, and suggests something missing. The autobiographical writings in general are honest, but curiously empty of love, or any strong emotion capable of releasing the writer from his spectatorial attitude. The boy's pleasure in nature alone provides joy, and it has to be said that the prose as a whole expresses, and partially analyses, an emotionally retarded condition.

When Edward Thomas applies his aesthetic and mythological imagination to people, the results can be particularly disturbing. In 'At a Cottage Door', in *Rest and Unrest* (1910), for example, he describes old women living in poverty in an industrial town in south Wales:

> Such creatures, chiefly women, were not uncommon. They were small, grey-skinned, with clotted grey hair; they had scarred faces, had lost an eye and most of their teeth; they wore soiled print or black dresses, bedraggled like the plumage of a dead bird in the mud and in colour approaching the foul dust of the pavement and the garbage of the gutter. In appearance they were genuine autochthons. This earth of flagstone, asphalte, granite, brick, iron, and ashes, might have protruded such a monstrous birth on a night of frost, to prove that it was not yet barren in its age and ignominy. One such crone crawling out into the light, unclean, dull and yet surprised, had a look as if she had just been exhumed; she might have been buried alive in the foundation of the town for luck, and had now emerged to see what had been done. (pp.113-114)

There is fascination and repulsion rather than compassion or anger here. There is also a suspect pleasure in arranging and interpreting the scene with little more sense of moral responsibility than if it were a landscape. The narrator (whose viewpoint is evidently the author's) combines observation of social fact with myth-making, and the most disturbing feature of the description is its unconscious cruelty. Above all, the writing simplifies. This tendency is increased by the perception of people in bird imagery, and contrast between them and the singleness of birds, which, according to Catherine Anne, "are not all tangled up and darkened with a number of things" (p.103). The related aestheticism and myth-making produce, at the end of the story, a mystifying vision of humanity as a "demon", which obscures both the narrator's attitude, (which is more complex and interesting than the above quotation reveals) and the town's social and historical formation.

Edward Thomas claimed to have "no historic sense", but, in the same book, *The South Country*, gave a fine illustration of it, applied to landscape:

> In some places history has wrought like an earthquake, in others like an ant or mole; everywhere, permanently; so that if we but knew or cared, every swelling of the grass, every wavering line of hedge or path or road were an inscription, brief as an epitaph, in many languages and characters. (p.155)

He goes on, however, to claim that we are like Taliesin, who was present in many times and places: "We belong to the days of Wordsworth, of Elizabeth, of Richard Plantagenet, of Harold, of the earliest bards" (p.156). This is the belief to which we owe 'Lob', and what Raymond Williams calls "a version of history which succeeds in cancelling history".[10] Thomas calls the experiences resembling Taliesin's "these many folds in our nature". He says "the face of the earth reminds us" of these, "and perhaps, even where there are no more marks visible upon the land than there were in Eden, we are aware of the passing of time in ways too difficult and strange for the explanation of historian and zoologist and philosopher. It is this manifold nature that responds with such indescribable depth and variety to the appeals of many landscapes" (p.157). Clearly, interiority, psychological depth, not history, is Edward Thomas's imaginative domain. The idea of the "manifold nature" is a stage in his long struggle to transcend the limitations of isolation and subjectivity and to connect himself with others. Although he never fully developed or embodied the idea, except, perhaps, in 'Lob', the "difficult and strange ways" in which he was aware of time dominate the poetry.

In his country books, Edward Thomas frequently discovers places of solitude and safety, which he sees as fragments of Eden or the Golden Age. This was a widespread literary preoccupation in England in his time and his persistence with it, which shows his strong need of the paradisal myth, calls to mind John Cowper Powys, who developed it into a whole complex imaginative world during a long lifetime. In Thomas's case, too, there is more to be said about the mythological imagination than that it cancels history. But in my view, that needs to be said first. Here, for example, is a sentence from *In Pursuit of Spring*: "I confess I did not think about the lad who was hanged for a hare when I caught sight of the church at Orcheston St. George, but rather of some imaginary, blissful time which at least lacked our tortures, our great men, our shame and conscience" (pp.158-159). Conscience is not, perhaps, so easily disposed of. But, even after the outbreak of war, Thomas was still capable of finding, in 'The Manor Farm', "a season of bliss unchangeable" awakened from Merry England.

In the short stories and sketches gathered together in *Rest and Unrest* and *Light and Twilight*, and in his novel, *The Happy-Go-Lucky Morgans*, Edward Thomas found a partial form of the self-expression which he found completely in his poetry alone. The fiction is concerned mainly with the paradisal myth, which may be summed up in these words from *The South Country*: "As mankind has looked back to a golden age, so the individual, repeating the history of the race, looks back and finds one in his own past" (p.131). One example must suffice of how he fictionalises this theme in his stories.

For Alice Lacking in 'The First of Spring', (*Rest and Unrest*), spring renews an aspiration, "a strong but vague and wordless desire to be something other than she was, to do something other than she was doing or had ever done" (p.8). Looking back from her present discontent, she recalls her childhood: "she remembered simply the bliss which she had in those days not recognised" (p.12). In her youth, when she had written poetry, she had carried "a secret" within her. It was "her personality, her self, what made her the equal of all men and things". Then, "she and her mother possessed the world" (p.13). But in growing older she lost her secret, her identity became uncertain and diffused, and the state of wholehearted being gave way to the divisions and discontents of self-consciousness. Alice's aspiration is now projected on to the spring and her desire to adopt a child, as an unconscious compensation for the child she has lost in growing older. But her wishes are frustrated, and the story ends ironically:

> "I think, Alice," said Colonel Lacking that evening, "you had better have a sea voyage. We will take one together, I think. Yes. This English spring is too much for us when we are no longer young. You're looking a fright."
>
> "It's not the spring, father, it's myself."
>
> "Where shall it be?" he continued, looking at a map of this world. (p.26)

In spite of the wooden dialogue, the story establishes the significance of the commonplace statement, "It's not the spring, father, it's myself" and the sense in which the spring is "too much" for Alice. No place on the map can indicate the lost world of childhood, which is, for her, more real than "this world".

The episodic *The Happy-Go-Lucky Morgans*, too, is about the possession, or loss, of a spiritual kingdom, which is usually identified with a period of unselfconscious childhood. The episodes are connected by the Morgans' house in Balham, and by the characters revolting against suburban constraint who gather there, and yearn romantically for "a larger air", which is contained in the past or in exotic legends or dreams. Here, again, is the "country" of childhood, found by Arthur and Philip in the woods and fields near London, and called by them "Our Country". It is a real place, but exists now in Arthur's memory as a state of being, a "Palace of the Mountain of Clouds", where boys are safe and solitary, "separated by great distances and great enchantment from the rest of the world" (p.39). Another character, Mr. Torrance, dwells on "the real world" in his mind, which is the place where he lived as a child; his writings and actual life have no connection with it. In this respect, he is one of Edward Thomas's most significant self-projections. David Morgan, a mystic who isolates himself in his 'Folly' in Wales, and dies there, is another. He is a man who has severed all bonds, except that with his wife, and crossed all the boundaries of human identity in his search for God. All the characters are 'innocents', and the novel is entirely without adult relationships or developed emotions. The Morgans' Abercorran House is a boy's paradise, and a refuge in which the various misfits find a physical and imaginative life that feeds their starved minds and senses; but it is itself a reflection of a more distant ideal, the place in Wales from which it is named. Glen Cavaliero, in his introduction to a new edition of the novel, makes a strong case for it, and says it is "pervaded by a tartness that prevents it from smacking in any way of compensatory fantasy".[11] It does indeed contain some impressive writing, especially in descriptions of the suburbs, but while I recognise that Edward Thomas is self-consciously critical of his own romanticism, I see the novel as far more of an indulgence of his escapism than Glen Cavaliero does. There is, however, one particularly interesting chapter, which indicates Thomas's subsequent development.

In Chapter XV, Mr. Stodham speaks for England:

> "England made you, and of you is England made.... Having denied England and your father and mother, you may have to deny your own self, and treat it as nothing, a mere conventional boundary, an artifice, by which you are separated from the universe and its creator. To unite yourself with the universe and the creator, you may be tempted to destroy that boundary of your own body and brain, and die. He is a bold man who hopes to do without earth, England, family, and self." (p.123)

In *The South Country* Thomas had looked back to "England, that swan's nest, that island which a man's heart was not too big to love utterly", and contrasted it with present-day "Great Britain, the British Empire, Britons, Britishers, and the English-speaking world", in which "he is fortunate who can find an ideal England of the past, the present, and the future to worship, and embody it in his native fields and waters or his garden, as in a graven image" (p.75). In *The Country* he had written: "I wonder how many others feel the same, that we have been robbed...of the small intelligible England of Elizabeth and given the word Imperialism instead" (p.6). The chapter about English patriotism in *The Happy-Go-Lucky Morgans* expresses something of the complexity of the issue as it affects a writer with a love of England *and* Wales, and in a confused and divided society. Nevertheless, what Mr. Stodham affirms, Edward Thomas was soon to practise. This is evident in his wartime essays, (later included in *The Last Sheaf*, 1928), 'England', 'Tipperary', 'It's a Long, Long Way', and 'This England', and in his poems.

Earlier, Edward Thomas had tended either to picture landscape aesthetically, or to dissolve it in evocations of Eden or the Golden Age. Then, his concern was with atmosphere and essence, but now it is with word and thing, and he accepts the "boundary" marked by "earth, England, family, and self". Thus, in 'This England', he conveys a sharper sense of a particular corner of England, in Herefordshire, than he had in earlier voluminous descriptions of landscape. His mind and mood are concentrated, in part, no doubt, because of the friendship with Robert Frost, which both enabled him to communicate freely at a deep level, and confirmed his ideas about the relation between style and speech, and in part because now, in wartime, as he says in 'England', "the whole land is suddenly home" (p.108). The conclusion of 'This England' shows clearly that the essay originated from the same experience as his poem 'The sun used to shine':

> Then one evening the new moon made a difference. It was the end of a wet day; at least, it had begun wet, had turned warm and muggy, and at last fine but still cloudy. The sky was banded with rough masses in the north-west, but the moon, a stout orange crescent, hung free of cloud near the horizon. At one stroke, I thought, like many other people, what things that same new moon sees eastward about the Meuse in France. Of those who could see it there, not blinded by smoke, pain, or excitement, how many saw it and heeded? I was deluged, in a second stroke, by another thought, or something that overpowered thought. All I can tell is, it seemed to me that either I had never loved England, or I had loved it foolishly, aesthetically, like a slave, not having realized that it was not mine unless I were willing and prepared to die rather than leave it as Belgian women and old men and children had left their country. Something I had omitted. Something, I felt, had to be done before I could look again composedly at English landscape, at the elms and poplars about the houses, at the purple-headed wood-betony with two stiff pairs of dark leaves on a stiff stem, who stood sentinel among the grasses or bracken by hedge-side or wood's-edge.

> What he stood sentinel for I did not know, any more than what I had got to do. (pp.220-221)

It would be absurd to make a qualitative comparison between the essay and the poem, but it may be observed that the prose is without the poem's somewhat conventional ending, where everything fades into memory and a sense of mortality dominates the mood. The prose, like the poem, has mystery, and, at the same time, is clear-cut with the edge of decision, which both arises from the concentrated mind and confirms it. Thomas possesses both himself and the land, but the possession is dependent on his willingness to sacrifice his life. He is no longer an isolated sensibility, free of a landscape which he can rearrange aesthetically at will or whim. The moon is not a poetic symbol of vague mystery or the spectator's solitude. It is "the same new moon" standing over the battlefield, the moon that will make "many other people" in England think of what it sees. "The purple-headed wood-betony", "stiff" and "sentinel", stands at once for sexual potency, protective love, and the acceptance of death. It is not, I think, a conscious comprehensive symbol; rather, its meaning arises from that "something that overpowered thought", by which Thomas, moved to his depths, is at once taken out of himself and gathered together, resting his being on the country he is prepared to die for. Written in September 1914, two months before the first poems, 'This England' reveals the whole man in a landscape to which he is decisively, substantially, related, and in which he shares common human bonds. Without this reality to rest upon, Edward Thomas could not express himself as a poet, and neither could he voice more than a baseless and incomplete self in his prose.

Notes

1. All quotations from Edward Thomas's prose are from first editions, with the exception of the following books: *Oxford* (1922), *Wales* (1924), *The Heart of England* (Open-Air Library, J.M. Dent, 1932), *The South Country* (J.M. Dent, 1932), *The Happy-Go-Lucky Morgans* (The Boydell Press, 1983).
2. *The Childhood of Edward Thomas* (1938), p.102.
3. *Ibid.*, p.134.
4. In a notebook, 31 August 1899. Quoted in R. George Thomas, *Edward Thomas: A Portrait* (1985), p.80.
5. *The South Country*, p.7.
6. Walter Pater, *The Renaissance*, Conclusion.
7. In a letter of 10 January 1915. Quoted in Eleanor Farjeon, *Edward Thomas: The Last Four Years* (1958), p.110.
8. "You see the central evil is self-consciousness carried as far beyond selfishness as selfishness is beyond self denial, ...and now amounting to a disease and all I have got to fight it with is the knowledge that in truth I am not the isolated

selfconsidering brain which I have come to seem — the *knowledge* that I am something more, but not the belief that I can reopen the connection between the brain and the rest." Edward Thomas, in a letter to Eleanor Farjeon, in 1913. Quoted in *Edward Thomas: The Last Four Years*, p.13.

9. Review of *North of Boston*, 22 July 1914; in *A language not to be betrayed*, ed. Edna Longley, p.125.
10. Raymond Williams, *The Country and the City* (1973), p.257.
11. *The Happy-Go-Lucky Morgans* (1983), Introduction, p.xi.

DICK DAVIS

'The Truth or Nothing': Edward Thomas's Literary Criticism

'The Truth or Nothing': Edward Thomas's Literary Criticism

The picture of Thomas which we receive from the poems of his last three years is that of a solitary, observant wanderer in the English countryside; if other men's books are present in his consciousness they exist as a slight precipitate, the ghost of an influence (Hardy in 'The New House', Frost in 'Up in the Wind'), perhaps a part of that undefined disabling confusion from which we see him painfully, relievedly working himself free. And yet for virtually his whole adult life, from his leaving Oxford in 1900 until his enlistment in 1915, he made his living as a commentator on other men's books, as a reviewer and writer of literary criticism. This entailed enormous and almost unremitting labour; rarely can anyone's mind have been more full of other men's writings and the necessity to form judgements on them:

> You don't know what it means to make £5 or £6 a week by reviewing. This week for example, I read review books all day on Monday and Tuesday, interrupted only by my little lots of housework, lessons to Merfyn and meals. Then until tonight I have been reading and writing all day with the same interruptions.... Original writing I dream about....
>
> (Letter to Gordon Bottomley)

He produced nine books of literary criticism (*Richard Jefferies*, *Feminine Influence on the Poets*, *Maurice Maeterlinck*, *Algernon Charles Swinburne*, *George Borrow*, *Lafcadio Hearn*, *Walter Pater*, *Keats*, *A Literary Pilgrim in England*) between 1909 and his death in 1917 — this at the same time that he was regularly writing reviews (chiefly of new poetry) for newspapers and periodicals. In his Introduction to *Letters from Edward Thomas to Gordon Bottomley* (1968), his biographer R. George Thomas attempts to compute how much criticism Thomas managed to produce, and arrives at a figure of:

> a minimum of 1,122 reviews — just over a million words about twelve hundred books. During the first four years (1900-1903) he averaged eighty reviews a year and in 1913-14 — when his daily reviewing slackened off and he was writing four or five books annually — he wrote only sixty full length reviews. So that between the Christmases of 1905 and 1912 he was

> contributing a hundred signed (or full length) reviews annually to the *Daily Chronicle* or the *Daily Post* (or to both), to the *Nation*, the *Athenaeum*, the *Academy*, or the *English Review*, besides at least fifty shorter notices to weeklies and, after 1907, a monthly article or two column unsigned review to the *Bookman*. The output is staggering...

It would be even more staggering if all of this critical prose were consistently interesting, intelligent and well-written, and it should be no surprise to learn that much of Thomas's criticism is repetitious, overwritten and simply tired — the reader feels the jadedness of Thomas's mind, the effort to be bright and sharp (in much of the earlier work the effort to be dim and florid), his awareness of an editor's desire for a defining judgement on something hardly worth defining or judging. The reader is reminded of Berlioz's remark about his own tedious search for the words that will define the difference between a ninth rate and a tenth rate composer.

But it is not merely a sense of tiredness, of an exhausted because too insistently called upon sensibility, that makes much of Thomas's prose less than a pleasure to read. If this were the case the later books and articles would not be as fresh and interesting as the earlier ones, and almost exactly the reverse is true. Of the critical books listed above perhaps only the last, *A Literary Pilgrim in England*, can now be read through with enjoyment and without irritation. Though there are many fine moments in the others they all contain passages of fustian, of writing on an automatic pilot set for the lofty and inspecifically beautiful. All of Thomas's poetry belongs to a period when he had thought carefully and at length about diction, and when he was conscious of friends and models who, while not dictating to him, could by their example indicate the kind of simplicity and clarity he by then wanted; most of his prose precedes this period and its models are not so much Frost and Hardy as Lamb and Pater.

Lamb's prose, its whimsy and plangency, its deliberate childishness and mock pedantries about trivia, would seem to have been evolved largely as a way of guarding Lamb against the appalling psychological truths in the midst of which he was forced to live: almost nothing serious can be said in such a style, and if something serious is inadvertently said it immediately dissolves in ironies and tearful little sighs. In Lamb's case the style is defensive, but in that of his innumerable late nineteenth century imitators it comes to seem smug and complacent, clubby and pompous. And with Pater too — as Thomas himself was to realise and point out — the defensive, artificial surface, the brilliant sheen, is all: neither author writes in a way that facilitates the apprehension of a truth, that weighs, judges and decides; they prefer to be evocative rather than exact, seductive rather than incontrovertible. The implication is that nothing solid or true can be articulated, and to attempt to do so is bad taste. The cultivation of sensibility — either sentimental in Lamb's case or eclectically aesthetic in Pater's — becomes an end in itself, and the outside world is regarded, is admitted to exist, only in so far as it feeds this sensibility. The legacy of such writing lies very heavily on Thomas's early work (as it does on that of many of his contemporaries), and even in his latest prose it is still discernible; his article 'Reviewing: an unskilled Labour' (1914) contains the sentence "But the only thing to be said for it is that it produces money, which produces food and clothing for aged parents, fair wives, innocent children", and it is difficult to come on the adjectives here without wincing.

In general though, such writing decreased as Thomas got older; a small but indicative sign is the way that he gradually substituted the "we" of his earlier criticism ("We are left to wonder why..." (1902), "We have no hesitation in saying..." (1902)) — the rather narcissistic "we" of a self-approving sensibility — with "you" in his later work; ("The others are more or less certainly to be identified if you wish" (1917) — he is talking about the originals for Jefferies's characters, or "You see that he [Hardy] is, as he says, exhibiting Wessex to us" (1917), in which the "us" definitely includes the imagined interlocutor "you"). The sensibility no longer conceives of itself as living in Huysmans-like solitude, but as a man speaking to men.

Thomas's critical prose is vast and amorphous in extent; he wrote of another equally voluminous and uneven writer, George Borrow, "He is best when he is without apparent design. As a rule if he has a design it is too obvious: he exaggerates, uses the old-fashioned trick of reappearance and recognition, or breaks out into heavy eloquence of description or meditation" and the words are equally true of Thomas himself. The grand design eludes him and he rarely tries for it. He was not a reviewer by accident — a review's brevity suited him, and his longer works often read like reviews strung together and awkwardly eked out. He deals in individual moments, in specifics, in sharp details and anecdotes, and it is this vivid particularity and individuality that he looks for in the works and writers he discusses. He is best in moments, and this seems right as his interest is so often in the momentary, anecdotal and fleeting.

He looks for uniqueness, for personality in fact, although he can feel ambivalent about doing so. He writes of A.C. Bradley, "he has given us the very deep and unusual pleasure of watching his thought facing its subject honestly"; of Arthur Symons, "lurking behind...and giving its unique quality to the book is this unexpressed personality and taste which, we feel, is far finer than anything he can say"; of Hudson "[he]...never paints a bird without showing the hand and the heart that paints it. It reveals the author in the presence of birds"; of Gilbert White, "We are always pleasantly conscious of the man in his style..." and he loves ballads for "those things which show us the heart of one man who stands out by himself" while Dampier's prose gives him "a very pleasant sense of the man himself".

As is apparent from the examples he gives, this individuality of phrase which seems revelatory of the man himself can be found in all periods of literature, but it seems to Thomas to be a particularly emphatic characteristic of contemporary writing; "It is hard to find one new and common element in modern books. But if such is to be found it is the assertion of the individuality of the individual". This personal, irreducible quiddity, the mark of a particular mind which might be imitated but not reproduced, is what elicits his approval. But it is an approval hedged about with conditions; he says of De La Mare, "The personal quality is intense and consistent, but it has no obvious egotism, no significant first person singular, no confession, defiance, lament, or hinted mystery". If he likes the personal he does not like the egotistical, the individual note has to be struck unself-consciously – to try for it is to become affected or vainly wordy; in defining what is wrong with Lafcadio Hearn's work he says "the personality of the writer is in his best work shown by his abnegation of personality".

The writers he champions — particularly the writers from the past — tend to be figures who have been thought to be not quite central to the history of English poetry — poets like Clare, Chatterton, Cowper; highly individual, slightly marginal figures, often failures whose tragic lives lend their works a particular pathos. And in the same way that he seeks out the modest, local and quirky he distrusts the public grand manner; he is better on Burns than on Tennyson, and he clearly distrusts Milton — for Thomas the grand manner equals hypocrisy and he virtually accuses Milton of this:

> Milton insists much upon the "naked beauty" of Eve, "undecked save with herself" and "no veil she needed, virtue proof", and "Eve ministered naked". He is also fond of pointing out that she felt no "dishonest shame", and that "no thought inferior altered her cheek", that "Love unlibidinous reigned", that she received Adam's courtship with "innocence and virgin modesty" — phrases which seem to show that the opposite was in his mind, and at least have the effect of suggesting the opposite to the reader; the poet himself is, as it were, a seventeenth-century intruder upon the scene, and really gives some indecency to the nakedness....

and he calls both Adam and Eve in 'Paradise Lost' "imperfectly visualized and resting too much upon the traditional or conventional view".

Thomas's criticism tends to look for the man behind the poetry as much as at the poetry itself; he says of Clare "no one reads him but loves him" — *him*, the man as much as the poetry. His essays on individual poets — and he clearly thinks of poets rather than poems as the realities he is dealing with — are full of biographical and topographical detail, and he will quote as much from letters and memoirs as from poems in his search for the elusive particularity of a man's life. For him the memorable and quotable moments in a man's poetry are usually details revelatory of some intimate and closely observed physical reality. 'Real' is perhaps his most unequivocally commendatory adjective, as when he says of a passage in Morris, "The water is real water", or of a line of Clare "The elder-tree occurs with exact reality", or of a line in Herrick "The cat too is very real" (he also wrote of Herrick "Perhaps he was short-sighted, for he seems to see very clearly little things which he could not have seen at all without special attention"); and the same quality attracts him in Crabbe's descriptions, of one of which he writes "how resolute is its avoidance of adding to the mystery by artifice". Such honesty before particular, local realities is supremely valuable to him, and he attempts to as it were repay the authors he loves by his concern for their own unique particularity.

Gradually this instinct for particularity, for the unique individual who records the specifics of his own experience with modest but as nearly absolute fidelity as is possible, became the defining impulse of Thomas's prose; the rather narcissistic 'prose-poetry' of the earlier descriptive works (much of his *Richard Jefferies* for example consists of Thomas being lyrical about things Jefferies had already been lyrical about) became less evident. The truth-finding impulse replaced reverie and verbose evocation; the end of this process is apparent in his poetry, though here it has become much swifter and has already been largely worked through in the prose.

When discussing his contemporaries he is much less concerned to celebrate the quirky and obscure; here the desire is much more to push into prominence what is striking and special — he does not make a cult of the minor, as he is sometimes ready to do when discussing poets from the past. He is convincing on the early poetry of both Yeats and Lawrence (Yeats was widely championed, this was not so of Lawrence) and he was instrumental in securing W.H. Davies a wide readership. He consistently praised De La Mare and all but worshipped W.H. Hudson. When Thomas was a child and an adolescent, Swinburne was considered to be the great modern poet, and it is particularly difficult for a critic to deal judiciously with an inflated reputation that has been created largely by his parents' generation; Thomas is accurate, and wittily accurate too, about Swinburne ("he kept as it were a harem of words, to which he was constant and absolutely faithful", and he shrewdly points out that Swinburne's all-purpose commendatory epithet is "bright", a trick that Pound imitated).

But it is his judgements of Pound himself, and of Frost, which are perhaps the most interesting, and which indicate how acute he was as a critic of contemporary verse.

He was unequivocal in his recognition of Pound's talent, seeing in *Personae* "a new writer [who] is good and in a new way", and he wrote of *Exultations of Ezra Pound* "It is a relief to us to turn from all but meaningless suavity and skill to something that appears to be individual". It was the peremptory, highly individual tone of Pound's early work (which he said made *Personae* "rather prickly to handle at first") which struck him, and he honoured Pound for it. Thomas recognised Pound's irritating idiosyncracies but they did not blind him to the fact that his voice was new and not to be ignored; "For brusque intensity of effect we can hardly compare them [the poems in

Personae] with any other work. Of course, this is due partly to his faults and to his pride in revolt, to his lack of all mere amiability, to his austerity, to his abruptness as of a swift beetle that suddenly strikes your cheek and falls stunned with its own force...". The faults that went with such aggressive individuality were perceptively defined; "It [*The Spirit of Romance*] is restlessly opinionated. He has, or desires to have, an opinion upon everything; and if he has not then his eccentric speech makes it appear that he has. He relies, in fact, as much upon his personality as upon his learning", and Thomas closed one review on a cautionary note that is alarmingly prophetic in view of Pound's subsequent career; "If he is not careful he will take to meaning what he says instead of saying what he means".

He was impressed by Pound's work and had reservations about it, but Frost's poetry was a major discovery for him and he seems to have seen it as an indication of the new direction he felt poetry needed. His friendship with Frost was of course instrumental in his own turning to poetry, and though the influence should not be exaggerated Thomas's blank verse is certainly much closer to Frost's blank verse than to anyone else's. His reviews of *A Boy's Will* and *North of Boston* are almost wholly positive; the subject matter is close to his own interests — the lives of solitary largely inarticulate people in rural settings — the lack of rhetorical flourish in Frost is close to his own later preference for direct, unadorned language; above all he approves of Frost's speaking tone, which he links with that of Wordsworth. The modesty he senses in Frost's work (whether Frost was really modest or not is neither here nor there) draws him too, "Nor is there any brag or challenge about this", as does the poetry's understated but always palpably present intensity, "But they [Frost's lines] are bound together and made elements of beauty by a calm eagerness of emotion". The phrase "a calm eagerness of emotion" recalls Thomas's brother's description of the way Thomas read verse aloud, "He read in an almost unaccentuated monotone, slowly, clearly...", and this alert passivity, this attentiveness to what is actually there, rather than the rhetoric of the ego that uses material for its own glorification, was something he clearly thought he had found in Frost's verse. He was impressed by Pound's coruscating brags and challenges, but Frost's work seems to have corresponded to something deep in Thomas's own psyche — he looked for and thought he had found a peace and truth there which the flashier more outwardly impressive Pound could not provide.

There would seem to be something of a paradox in Thomas's preference for Frost to Pound: Pound's is after all the more obviously individual and idiosyncratic voice and it was individuality — a sense of this and no other man speaking — that Thomas looked for in poetry. The preference is partly explicable by the stronger 'reality' of Frost's verse, as against the obvious bookishness of Pound's, but it has also to do with exactly this problem of individuality.

Though Thomas was drawn to the individual voice as a sign of poetic life, of truth and originality rather than facility and imitation, he was also profoundly suspicious of the way individuality, and an excessive consciousness of individuality, seemed to be the defining characteristic of so much contemporary verse. He wrote of Chaucer, "He did not assert himself because he was not so cut off from his audience that he was bound to do so" and it is impossible not to hear a note of regret in this formulation. For Thomas the modern writer is a solitary — as Thomas always called himself — cut off from his audience, and it is this that accounts for his self-conscious individuality. But though Thomas saw himself as a solitary it is clear that he longed for community; the patriotism of his poetry is an expression of this longing, as is the way — in both prose and poetry — he savours the moment of entering an inn and being welcomed there, "the inn where all were kind,/ All were strangers". The feeling is particularly strong in 'The Owl' which begins with Thomas as an outsider who is welcomed into the inn's community but then forced by the owl's cry to think of those still excluded, so that he imaginatively enters the community of the excluded solitaries, "Soldiers and poor, unable to rejoice". His ideal in verse would seem to have been a voice that treated of the inarticulate community — often a community of the ignored or despised — a voice which achieved individuality almost in spite of itself (as in the work of Burns, Clare and Crabbe, all poets of whom he wrote with particular affection and insight); such a poet does not make himself — the furniture of his own cluttered consciousness — his subject; he leaves behind what Thomas called "the central evil...self-consciousness" and becomes an individual voice merely by virtue of innate talent and a perceptive sympathy of mind.

Thomas's feeling for landscape is closely bound up with his sense of solitariness and of "self-consciousness" as "the central evil": it is clear that he sought in the contemplation of landscape the kind of self-loss which human company could not give him — he wrote to Gordon Bottomley that "with me, social intercourse is only an intense form of solitude, and...solitude is what I have to avoid". But as H. Coombes has pointed out, landscape, the anatomising of nature, could not finally give him the solace he sought: "Thomas's sense of 'otherness' in nature, that quality or aspect which in its independence and utter apartness from human life makes a strange and often powerful and disturbing impact on the *human* mind, was deep and lifelong". As Thomas himself put it, "I am not a part of nature. I am alone." Coombes compares Thomas's apprehension of "the immense dark force" in nature to Conrad's perception of the natural world as immeasurably alien and destructive: a closer parallel, because like Thomas he too at first sought self-loss in the contemplation of nature, is with the American poet Yvor Winters. Winters came to see the attempt to lose the self in a kind of ecstatic contemplation of or communion with nature (as Thomas admired in the work of Jefferies) as an invitation to madness and suicide; Winters's nature was Conradian in its vast indifference to man, and the man who attempted empathy or union with it would be destroyed. Winters recorded the sense of terror which this apprehension induced in him in his short story 'The Brink of Darkness': the crucial moment occurs when the protagonist stares out through a window onto a blank moonlit snow-covered landscape; there is an extraordinarily similar moment in Thomas's autobiographical novel *The Happy-Go-Lucky Morgans*, in which a young child "pressed his face on the pane to see the profound of deepening night.... The abyss of solitude below and around was swallowing the little white moon and might swallow me also; with terror at this feeling I turned away...".

'The Brink of Darkness' would be an excellent title for much of Thomas's best work in both poetry and prose, though the terror is often muted and the threatened loss of identity is more desired than feared. Again and again in his poems he traces a sensation, a line of thought, back to a point where he can no longer articulate what it is he is following and he is left with "Only an avenue, dark, nameless, without end". His mind cannot close on the elusive quiddity he seeks, "I cannot bite the day to the core", and typically *The Childhood of Edward Thomas* opens with the sentence "When I penetrate backward into my childhood I come perhaps sooner than many people to impassable night". This awareness of the hidden origins of what haunts and moves him is beautifully presented in the last stanza of his poem 'It rains';

> on its fine stalk
> Twilight has fined to naught, the parsley flower
> Figures, suspended still and ghostly white,
> The past hovering as it revisits the light.

The image was obviously important to him — he records it in *The Heart of England* where he writes of "the ghostly white cow-parsley flowers suspended on unseen stalks". The impulse is the same in the best of his critical writing — the parsley-flower is the work the poet leaves behind him and which we can read, it is "The past hovering as it revisits the light", but the invisible stalk on which the flower rests is what intrigues Thomas, and his nagging consciousness of it feeds his desire to trace back the work through memoir, biography and local topographical detail. The phrases "a sort of", "a kind of" recur often in his critical writing and are an indication of the way he feels that what he is dealing with must elude him — the stalk finally stays unseen — they are the signature of his frustrated truth-searching. When he wrote in 'The Chalk Pit' "I should prefer the truth/ Or nothing" he had already chosen "nothing" because he knew "the truth" to be impossibly elusive.

Thomas was never an academic and he was very suspicious of the academic appropriation of literature: most literary criticism is now written by academics and it would be strange if Thomas's *ad hoc* and very *ad hominem* approach to literary texts had had much influence on subsequent literary criticism. But the values he celebrated have I believe passed into academic debate, largely through the work of the Leavises. If we read Thomas on Jefferies for example, we might be reading one of the Leavises:

> ...in all his best writing...his seriousness, his utter frankness, the obvious importance of the matter to himself, give us confidence in following him.... He is on the side of health, of beauty, of strength, of truth, of improvement in life to be wrought by increasing honesty, subtlety, tenderness, courage, and foresight...

The enthusiasm may be unscholarly and intemperate, but the values are the same and it is not surprising that both Leavises found much to praise in Thomas's writings.

But his chief influence as a critic has been outside the academy; in his insistence on biographical and topographical detail — his insistence on setting a writer not only in his landscape but among his family and friends — in his love for the minor and neglected, in the robustness and occasionally aggressive anger of his concern for Englishness and the nature of English writing, in his sudden tendernesses and irritations, above all in his insistence on the speaking voice as a mark of individuality and in his genuine and obvious love for the poets he celebrates, the spirit of his criticism has continued to live in two writers — Geoffrey Grigson and C.H. Sisson; both mavericks who have read widely and without regard for the pressures of an academic 'field' or specialisation, both non-academics who are passionate in their likes and dislikes, both in the best true sense amateurs of poetry.

JOHN PIKOULIS

Edward Thomas as War Poet

Edward Thomas as War Poet

One of the signal features of Robert Frost criticism has been the development of the view that, far from being a benign poet of rustic matters, he was one who had been "acquainted with the night". Yet, despite the marked similarity in temperament between Thomas and Frost and the critical role Frost played in Thomas's emergence as a poet, no such development has occurred in Edward Thomas criticism. Rather the reverse: everyone has been ready to assure us that his 'melancholia' was a fitful matter in his progress to self-knowledge and poetry, ended by a soldier's accidental death at Arras in 1917. In this account, Thomas's prose works expressed, at first flowerily but with a growing precision and sensitivity, a vision of England which he converted to poetry when he found the appropriate language to express it in the appropriate circumstances.

In fact, Thomas's progress was very different, and the clue to it has been with us all these years in the person of Alun Lewis who, as a young volunteer of twenty-five, was posted to the Royal Engineers No.1 Railway Training Centre at Longmoor in Hampshire, a few miles from Steep and Wick Green where Thomas spent his most fruitful years as a poet.

> I have been garrisoned for six months in Edward Thomas's country and walked his walks. I have sheltered from the rain in the beautiful house he built but did not inhabit. I have read his poems often and often in tent and hut.

This comes from Lewis's review of Thomas's *The Trumpet and Other Poems* in *Horizon* (III, 13, January 1941, pp.78 and 80). Together with 'To Edward Thomas' and 'All day it has rained...', it expresses Lewis's understanding of Thomas and it turns on one central quality:

> ...as a war poet, say that he did not suffer as Sassoon, Owen, Rosenberg, and was not embittered beyond bearing, but felt it as a voice in him — Death, the ultimate response that he, despite himself, desired.[1]

Lewis's earlier reference to the house Thomas "did not inhabit" (apparently a curious error, since Thomas did live in the house Geoffrey

Lupton designed for him) returns to the same point, for it refers to his psychological inability to share the house with his family. That is the meaning of his being "sensitive and somehow apart". He was one who felt 'a voice' calling him to Death, a voice he wished in part to resist but which proved to be a greater force on him than any other. As 'To Edward Thomas' puts it: "... I knew the voice that called you/ Was soft and neutral as the sky/ Breathing on the grey horizon, stronger/ Than night's immediate grasp, the limbs of mercy/ Oblivious as the blood". It was a voice that grew "clearer,/ More urgent": "all else dissolved away,/ — Projected books, half-thoughts, the children's birthdays,/ And wedding anniversaries as cold/ As dates in history — ...". This recoil from people, in Lewis's view, led to Thomas's end, which he phrased twice in concluding lines to poems in the same dramatic way: in 'To Edward Thomas' "Till suddenly, at Arras, you possessed that hinted land" (a line suggesting the pursuit of hidden treasure rather than accidental death), and in 'All day it has rained...' "where Edward Thomas brooded long/ On death and beauty — till a bullet stopped his song." It was not, as we know, a bullet but nonetheless death of a kind he had long brooded over, one interfused with beauty, Death and Beauty being his theme as it was to be Lewis's.

Both poem endings derive from Thomas, whose 'The Path' concludes: "till, sudden, it ends where the wood ends". Lewis's deliberate allusion to this poem retroactively assists our interpretation of it. It is the most informative kind of criticism. Thomas's line, in turn, derives from the last line of Keats's 'Bright star' sonnet: "And so live ever — or else swoon to death", a line he praised for the "break in the rhythm...as if life intruded — or, rather, death. This end of his poetry was fitting".[2] And we may say much the same of him.

Everything in Thomas turns on this recoil from love and friendship in favour of death. He himself described it in 'Rain', a symbolic property Lewis seized on for his 'All day it has rained...':

> Like me who have no love which this wild rain
> Has not dissolved except the love of death,
> If love it be towards what is perfect and
> Cannot, the tempest tells me, disappoint.

Still, sombre lines, converting a soldier's apprehension of death into a poet's inner conviction of it, his belief that it represents an ideal that washes him "cleaner than I have been/ Since I was born into this solitude". Thomas wrote of it in *The South Country*. It is, I think, the starting point for any Thomas criticism. A young Welsh boy goes for a walk with his father.

> [There] suddenly opened before me — like a yawning pit, yet not only beneath me but on every side — infinity, endless time, endless space; it was thrust upon me, I could not grasp it, I only closed my eyes and shuddered

> and knew that not even my father could save me from it, then in a minute it was gone. To a more blessed child some fair or imposing vision might have risen up out of the deep and given him a profounder if sadder eye for life and the world. How unlike it was to the mystic's trance, feeling out with infinite soul to earth and stars and sea and remote time and recognizing his oneness with them. To me, but later than that, this occasionally recurring experience was an intimation of the endless pale road, before and behind, which the soul has to travel; it was a terror that enrolled me as one of the helpless, superfluous ones on earth. (p.75)

Here is a signal experience, which the adult was later to identify with a sense of beauty racked by self-accusation and a profound feeling of worthlessness. In 'The Glory', the appeal of a summer morning summons the poet yet leaves him scorning "All I can ever do, all I can be" since he lacks the wisdom or strength to match nature. Before him "the pale dust pitted with small dark drops" (evocative language recalling the "small dark spot" of "The clouds that are so light" and the image of the endless road in *The South Country*). The poem ends on a note of frantic desperation: "I cannot bite the day to the core."

That was because Thomas had no core. We can speculate on the reasons for this, but the fact nonetheless remains. There is the well-attested presence of doubles in his work from first to last, figures which argue not only an unintegrated self but also the presence of an Other who represents the mortal self in peril. Thomas once described his depression as "a sort of conspiracy going on in [my head] which leaves me only a joint tenancy and a perpetual sense of the other tenant and wonder what he will do".[3] It was an acute burden and repeatedly he turned to nature and, to a lesser extent, his family and friends for comfort. But always he was thrown back on himself — he who had no self. It is a curious thing that his letters to his wife Helen from Oxford carry no signature. They are not broken off; they are detailed wholes full of loving reflections which bear no superscription or salutation — an alarming thought.

In the passage from *The South Country* I have just quoted, it is interesting to note the presence of Thomas's father, a notable achiever in politics and religion who undoubtedly contributed to his son's sense of futility. Estranged from him as from the parched family life he described in *The Childhood of Edward Thomas* (1938), Thomas married Helen Noble and the results were equally disastrous. Of course, anyone who has read Helen's memoirs and letters cannot fail to be moved by their shining devotion to Edward and her own warm, intelligent nature, so nearly broken by his death and so frequently tested by events before that. Yet it remains true, as Thomas well understood, that, responsive as he was, he could not be responsive enough. He could not return Helen and the children's love — not because he did not love them or because he loved elsewhere but because he could not love. Describing Edward to Janet Hooton as "bitter, hard, and impatient, quick to violent anger, and subject to long fits of depression"[4], Helen wrote: "He cannot love, Janet, he cannot respond to my love. How can he when all is so dark..."[5]. It is knowledge she could not often repeat later, for understandable reasons. But Edward did, in his epitaph in 'Beauty': "Here lives all that no one loved of him/ And that loved no one". In 'And you, Helen', he offers to give himself to her "if I could find/ Where it lay hidden and it proved kind". That his self should be an "it" detached from "I" is characteristic.

'No one so much as you' confesses Helen's love for Edward and his worthlessness before her:

> I but respond to you
> And do not love.
>
> ...
>
> I at the most accept
> Your love, regretting
> That is all: I have kept
> A helpless fretting
>
> That I could not return
> All that you gave
> And could not ever burn
> With the love you have,
>
> Till sometimes it did seem
> Better it were
> Never to see you more
> Than linger here
>
> With only gratitude
> Instead of love —

Helen affected to believe that this poem was addressed to Thomas's mother, though why a thirty-eight year old should reprove himself for not "burning" with love for his mother, whom he cradles as the isolated pine the dove, is not clear. Apparently Helen did not want to believe that the breach between her and Edward was final. In August, 1913, she wrote to Janet Hooton:

> He's tried hard during these last two years to kill my love for him but it's just the same as it always was, it's my great treasure, the thing that keeps me going.... Sometimes I think he does not love me any more, and my soul gets into a panic of terror, and then out of the darkness comes some wonderful gleam that gives me new hope....[6]

When Edward met Robert Frost in October 1913, he spoke obsessively about wanting to divorce Helen.[7]

No wonder the marriage was uneven: all the giving was on Helen's part, all the taking on Edward's. Yet he showed an acute sense of responsibility in providing for his family and was driven to frantic reviewing and bookmaking as a result, ironically itself to become an additional source of exasperation to him. In 'The Attempt' (*Light and Twilight* 1911), he tells of a man called Treharon's attempt to commit suicide in remorse for the suffering he causes his wife and daughter. He goes into the woods with a revolver, "called to death, but hardly to an act which could procure it". For him, death is "an idea tinged with poetry", promising release from "the hopeless search for something that would make it possible for him to go on living like anybody else without questioning". Treharon is about to bring the cartridge under the hammer when he is interrupted by the halloos of a stranger — not, it seems, directed at himself but "for his own delight".

> The cry rescued him...he raised the revolver and turned it to his breast, shut his eyes and touched the trigger, but too lightly.... For a moment he dreamed that he had succeeded. He saw the man who found him pick up the revolver and examine it. Finding but one cartridge in the chambers he concluded that the dead man was a person of unusual coolness and confidence, with an accurate knowledge of the position of the heart. (pp.172-3)

At that, Treharon returns home for tea, "thinking himself impenetrably masked". And so he is, as readers of Helen's account of the same episode in *World Without End* (1931) will recall.

This story conveys what I see as one of the most important decisions Thomas ever made, not quite conscious but deliberately so all the same. He knew he was to die and wished to die but accepted that he was not to kill himself; it would be done for him. Thus the double's intervention and the strange indecision as to whether Treharon has actually killed himself or not as he imagines the discovery of his body. As an earnest of his resolve, he goes through the motions and points the revolver at his breast, lightly touching the trigger. He has imaginatively anticipated himself and commits himself magically to death. All he will need to do is place himself in the right position at the right time and let fate have its way. Thomas was the reluctant or hesitant suicide, one who lacked the courage (or single-mindedness) to finish himself off and who found in the war a miraculous release from his private dilemma.

It is in this sense that we may think of him as a war poet, one who, at the end of 1914, suddenly discovered that external events mirrored his own inner disturbance, promising him the long-desired consummation. The release of his genius in poetry followed, not as a sign of increasing mental health but because he had at last found his direction. The end of his malady was in sight and he could put himself to creative use as never before. 'The Attempt' is by no means an isolated event. It reveals a continuing state of mind. In 1907,

Thomas again contemplated suicide, commenting, "It is dislike of the effort to kill myself and fear that I could not carry it through if I half did it that keeps me alive. Only that. For I hate my work, my reviewing: my best I feel is negligible: I have no vitality, no originality, no love. I do harm. Love is dead and lust almost dead. N.B. These thoughts have come to me at least once a week for three or four years now and frequently during the last seven — except as to lust".[8] From at least 1900 onwards, then, he was possessed by death. Even when Helen first knew him at seventeen, he was morbid and introspective. His moods became habitual after the crisis of 1902-3, when he spent "whole days doing absolutely nothing"[9], gripped by a nervous, irritable state:

> A continuous palpitation and sense of something approaching that never comes, prevents me from writing. I don't mean a sense of approaching good or bad luck, but merely a sense of *something* coming, as if I had heard a report and waited for the other barrel.[10]

Treharon couldn't have put it better.

> What I really ought to do is to live alone. But I can't find courage to do the many things necessary for taking that step. It is really the kind H. and the children who make life *impossible.*[11]

Physical exhaustion succeeded the nervous agitation as it was produced by it. By 1908, his depressions were coming once a month for a week or so. By the beginning of 1913, he confessed: "My health is now definitely bad, not a mere depression — and I don't know how it will develop".[12] That year, he decided to leave home and stayed away from October until the following February. When that failed I think he decided to divorce Helen.

What might have happened had the war not broken out we can never tell, though the very first poem he wrote in December, 1914, 'Up in the Wind', gives us a vivid portrait of his state of mind, relating as it does the bitterly miserable complaints of a woman trapped in a country inn high up in a beech wood, reminiscent of Thomas's own estrangement at Steep described later in 'The New House' and 'Wind and Mist'. But the war came and with it the soldier's engagement with death which he converted to his own private use. Unable to "bite the day to the core", unable to love, despising his own weakness, he came, like Keats — whom he wrote a book about that year —, "to choose death rather than life".[13] And that, I believe, is the crucial psychological mechanism that unlocked the poetry in him, thus enabling us to answer the most important critical question we can ask of Thomas: why did he start writing poetry so late? Why was all of it written during the war? There is nothing like it in literature for comparison. Just as Alun Lewis could not release the poetry within himself until the ghost of Thomas intervened, so Thomas had to wait for the meeting with his poetic double — Robert Frost

— at the outbreak of war before he could become a poet.

Frost was convinced that the war made "some kind of new man and a poet" out of Thomas.[14] Again, he believed the decision to enlist "helped him make the other decision to be a poet in form"[15]. Andrew Motion puts it this way:

> Because all his poetry was written after the outbreak of war, it is all, in an important sense, war poetry. Behind every line, whether mentioned or not, lies imminent danger and disruption.[16]

"Every line" overstates it somewhat, but the idea is more convincing than some assumed twenty-year-long development in self-understanding that bore the poetry as its fruit as after a happy gestation. Something more disruptive is needed, and we have it in *The Happy-Go-Lucky Morgans* (1913), where Thomas describes the furore of Mr. Stodham, a dull, middle-aged clerk who is visited by a Dryad in his study during an illness. This beautiful woman has "something to do with books" and he attends her anxiously as she gasps for breath. "Air," she cried, "Air — the wide air and light — air and light" '. (pp.170-1) Mr. Stodham opens or smashes every window in the house before making a bonfire in the middle of the drawing room and rushing out into the street "as if he were trying to escape himself — which he was"(p.173). He is a comic insurrectionary, Kubla Khan of the suburbs.

Thomas was truly a Muse poet, haunted by the goddess yet unable to reach her promised stillness, one which is akin to the perfection of beauty but, in fact, inseparable from the cessation of life, not the mystic's trance but a presage of annihilation. In *Light and Twilight*, he allies himself to "the universe" in a Richard Jefferies-like moment which transforms him into "something not to be separated from the dark earth and light sky, a strong citizen of infinity and eternity" (p.51). Thomas gave the name of "melancholy" to such "moments of everlastingness" when

> It was not happiness and powers
> Coming like exiles home again,
> And weakness quitting their bowers,
> Smiled and enjoyed, far off from men....

This is from 'The Other', and it describes the self-pursuit and mental harrassment which attends such moments of release. The spiritual self follows the social self until eventual surcease — and relief. It is important to notice the symbolism of inns in the early poems, matching that of forests. The inn is a temporary place of abode, a gathering of stray individuals, not a home.[17]

In 'The Queen of the Waste Lands' (*Rest and Unrest*, 1910) Thomas records a meeting with a woman who floats from the rain drops in a passing storm. She is the queen of the waste lands and sepulchres, "fuller of death even than the graves", "very placid in the eternal rain". He tells her he is anxious to join her. "Yet a little while," she replies, "and you shall have your will, though you cannot know it when the day comes. Farewell." (p.185) It is a variant of 'The Attempt', a Keatsian blending of love and death, and one more reason why such moments of repose in nature are "not happiness".

At the beginning of the poetry, Thomas emerges from the forest of his perplexity in 'The Other' and discovers the certainty of death in 'Old Man', a dark avenue, "nameless, without end" (the infinite road of *The South Country* again). This leads to 'The Signpost', another dialogue of self and other, which debates what he should do with his life before receiving his "mouthful of earth", a remedy for "all/ Regrets and wishes". In 'The Other', too, the man who chases "the unseen moving goal" finds nothing but "remedies/ For all desire". The poems that Thomas wrote in that first winter of 1914-1915 are truly storm-tossed, establishing the symbols of wind and rain. Hardly a poem is free of their effects as they release the pent-up crisis in him. Throughout, one thing is defined in terms of another: the sky through the mud, spring through winter, day and night through twilight, peace through storm, the self through the Other, death through life. It is a typical confusion of moods. At the end of 'The Other', the inner self discovers that the alter ego does not *want* the breach between them to be healed and will forever be at the mercy of the other. That discovery then yields, through the sequence of poems that follows, to 'Lights Out', one of the last poems, where the poet re-enters the forest — now converted into a metaphor of sleep — and finally loses "my way/ And myself".

The approach to death is punctuated by the "season of bliss unchangeable" first discovered in 'The Manor Farm', a relative of "moments of everlastingness", when the permanence of nature is revealed to one who observes from the "rock-like mud". ('Adlestrop' and 'Swedes' are variants of the same idea). Direct mentions of the war, obliquely referred to in 'After Rain', begin with 'A Private' — a variant of Hardy's 'Drummer Hodge' — and make more sensitive the appeal of nature to "what yet lives in me" ('Beauty'). The two are drawn together in 'May 23', a particularly fine day between tempests when Jack Noman disappears, a version of English Everyman who comes to reassure Thomas that the death of the individual nevertheless assures the immortality of the type.

The first of the poems called 'Home' is an especially frank avowal of the theme: "Not the end: but there's nothing more". All the seasons, all human relations, are as of nothing compared with "That land,/ My home, I have never seen;/ No traveller tells of it,/ However far he has been." Once more we meet the image of journeying. R. George Thomas has suggested that the home is the poet's childhood home in Balham, though he does not explain why Thomas is supposed never to have seen it and why it should remain outside the range of travellers however far they may have been. The Shakespearean echo makes it more likely that it is death, the beautiful country, a point so astutely seized on by Alun Lewis when he defined

Thomas's death at Arras as being his possession of "that hinted land".

The question Thomas poses here is: where should he go now that hope has gone? His answer recalls 'The Attempt': "I cannot go back,/ And would not if I could"; he must wait "Until blindness come". As the weary Other of *The South Country* says, "I dare not say I live.... I have no courage. I can at least endure.... I cannot look forward — there is nothing ahead — just as I cannot go back." (p.87) The road, as ever in Thomas, is "a symbol of mortal things with their beginnings and ends always in immortal darkness" (*The Icknield Way*, 1913,p.vii). To go back is to renew the promise of youth and this he abjures, feeling himself too captive of the past, too full of an "overblown immaturity" (*ibid.* p.140).

Exasperatedly, fascinatedly, he drifted to the end. Moments of joy remained, of course, most uncomplicatedly in 'March the 3rd', though usually with that confusion of moods that makes the material references in Thomas's poetry seldom less than ambivalent. The thread, however, was never lost and 'Will you come?' is a direct and passionate appeal to the Muse. By way of contrast, the moment out of time offers mystic-like glimpses of the beauty that remains in the days left: Merry England, Lob, fragments of art that survive man's passing. These are nearly always sadly regarded — until the more sombre symbols of rain and wind throw them into kindlier light. To leave one's mark on the countryside or literature by trying to save them from destruction and becoming "one of the lords of No Man's Land" — an ideal 'England' but also the trenches — offers a last chance to do something valuable. From this time on, Thomas's war became more personal with his decision to enlist in July, 1915.

Partly, this was taken under force of circumstance; partly it expressed a very clear determination, both social and imaginative, to express his love for things of worth, now so much more urgent to him. The reasons he gave himself in 'This is no case of petty right or wrong' are more than a little sentimental: few would suppose that *his* England of thrushes, poplars, barns and nettles would be much affected by a German victory. Thomas was taking his bearings, and the finest fruit of the process is 'Melancholy'. Here, again in wind and rain, he redefines melancholy not as a moment of "everlastingness" but as an impulse away from humanity. Though he does not know precisely what it is he desires, his unhappiness "sweeten[s] the strange sweetness". This magic moment, with its Coleridgean echoes — "soft as dulcimers, sounds of near water falling" — is identified with the imagination so that, more and more, poetry becomes a force that separates him from the old. (In *In Pursuit of Spring*, 1914, Thomas made much of the Coleridgean analogy, as I have discussed elsewhere.[18])

In 'Melancholy', Thomas surrenders "company". The "wisest" or "dearest" voice, "my friends, my foes, or me" are all discarded in favour of words, human relations now as "remote as if in history" (a concept richly re-employed by Alun Lewis in 'To Edward Thomas'). The poet luxuriates in the raving storm and a sense, defined in 'The Glory' a few days later, of having "naught to travel to". In 'The Word', he tells of having forgotten "so many things" that "once were much to me", all save the "pure thrush word" which is the voice of nature "out of the reach of change" ('Haymaking'). Even nature, however, begins to speak to him of his destiny in 'Fifty Faggots', where the chopped wood brings to mind the war, war's end and the ending of "many other things".

Even so, Thomas's nature poems from this time are his most relaxed and exercised a necessary steadying influence on him. "I shall be here some day again", he dreamed of telling Frost in a poem that is full of Romantic associations, 'A Dream', written shortly before his enlistment, where he finds some of nature's immortality for himself. Perhaps no suicide ever contemplates death without such an assurance. In 'Digging', his first post-enlistment poem, he tells of finding two clay pipes, one his own, one "perhaps" a soldier's from Marlborough's time (he had written the Duke's life earlier that year): two immortalities. Thereafter, in the poems of the second winter, the mood darkened considerably. These are less dramatic than the previous year's but also more ominous, alive to "moments of everlastingness" or seasons of "bliss unchangeable" but preoccupied with what is "ahead and behind" ('The Thrush'). The mood is described beautifully in 'Liberty', where poet and moon (as ever the Muse's light) stand over a grave, the poet "half in love" with pain, a Keatsian echo that greatly enriches the theme.

'Rain' shows again the grim recoil from people. Thomas's reference to those "whom once I loved" places his family ties firmly in the past. There is now "no love which this wild rain/ Has not dissolved"; the completeness of the gesture is striking. Especially in the context of 'This is no case of petty right or wrong' (the immediately preceding poem), it gives his joining the war a more compulsive complexion, and lends that poem's gentler phrases an unswerving conviction — and a longing. The mood expressed is familiar, as *The Icknield Way* shows (pp.280-3), where the double pronounces final judgement on Thomas that is compounded of isolation, weariness, self-recrimination and submission to fate.

The Muse was the only one who could solace him now, promising him beauty and a final consummation. The "endless road" has its particular goddess, as roads have always done, and "A language not to be betrayed", especially now that "all roads lead to France". In 'Roads', Thomas substitutes the company of the dead returning from the battlefront for lovingkindness. Writing to Helen about the poem, he wrote: "That Helen [of verse nine] is more real than the lady in the four verses [of 'Song' (2) who Helen feared was based on a real-life model]. Oh, you needn't think of another lady."[19] In a way, though, Helen was right. There had been a transference of affections: from her to the Muse.

Thomas's despair was now very great. In 'The Ash Grove', he pens a portrait of himself half-dead, like the trees, secure from the "spirits of memory" as from "fear", the past and the future. Even so, there was something in him "unwilling to die" and it shows the degree of conflict that went on in him as the ties loosened. Occasionally, he could even protest against the "stone-deaf and stone-blind" deity that demanded the soldier's sacrifice ('February Afternoon'). More prominent, though, are the poems of disengagement, those that expressed his hatred for his father and his alienation from Helen ('No one so much as you') and committed him to 'The Unknown' which lures him from his door (compare "dark within the door" in 'Liberty') to the moonlit moor.

The simple lack
Of her is more to me
Than others' presence,
Whether life splendid be
Or utter black.

Once more, the Muse appears, giver and taker of life, spirit of nature and dark visitant.[20]

In her company, Thomas prepared his farewells to his family (the so-called 'Household Poems'), though even she was to desert him in 'Go now'. In 'It rains', a development of the "moments of everlastingness" theme, he is "nearly as happy as possible" alone in the rain at twilight, thinking of the love that was: "never, never again,// Unless alone, so happy shall I walk/ In the rain." In 'The sun used to shine', another walk is described, the one he took with Frost in August, 1914. Everything has faded. In due course, others may walk their fields discussing men and poetry and war, looking at an apple fed on by wasps, "a sentry of dark betonies" and pale purple crocuses seemingly born in "sunless Hades fields". These subtle allusions to the war deepen the mood and provide the thread which links Herefordshire fields with Hades and the deathless ones of memory.

Thomas's end, as defined in 'No one cares less than I', is expressed in 'As the team's head brass', where he sits on a "fallen" elm watching a ploughman. The latter's fertile occupation contrasts with the "fallen" dead alluded to by the tree and the poet's silent identification with it. The fact that the tree was brought down by a blizzard on the night the ploughman's mate was killed in France intensifies the connection. In his conversation, the poet observes that he would not mind going to France himself if "I could only come back again", even at the cost of an arm, though if "I should lose my head, why, so,/ I should want nothing more" — a nicely ambiguous phrase. Then, "for the last time", he looks at the ploughman's "clods", an evocative image in the context of death which is further enhanced by "crumble", "topple over" and "stumbling" in the description of the latter's apparently life-enhancing activities. (The idea of seeing things for a last time is a favourite at this time: it appears in 'It rains', written just over a fortnight before, in 'I never saw that land before' the previous week, in 'It was upon' the following month and 'How at once...' the month after.) True, in 'As the team's head brass' there is some attempt to relate things ending with things beginning: the ploughman himself and the lovers who, by a Hardyesque coincidence, enter the woods and leave them at the end. But these are not for Thomas. He only has to notice them to detach himself from them now that he is "bound away for ever,/ Away somewhere, away for ever..../ I could not return from my liberty,/ To my youth and my love and my misery.// The past is the only dead thing that smells sweet..." ('Early One Morning').

Thomas applied for a commission in the Royal Artillery in June, 1916, shortly after these poems were written, and the fact that they all dwell on death provides us with a vivid picture of his state of mind at the time. He was not so much drifting towards death as placing himself before it. As Jan Marsh says of his decision to join the Artillery: "It was a virtually suicidal step: the survival rate on the Western Front was notoriously low."[21] Indeed, there was no pressing reason for a thirty-seven year old like Thomas to enlist at all but, having done so, there was no reason why he should have put in for a commission. Having done so there was no further reason why, in late 1916, he should have volunteered to go to France or why, at Arras as Assistant Adjutant at HQ, he should have asked to be relieved of staff duties and rejoin his battery, where he eventually died. These are compulsive actions deriving from the drama I have been outlining and performed with a truly great composure.

The Goddess now appeared bleak. Comparing a second spring with an earlier one in 'It was upon', Thomas cannot avoid summoning up deathly images. As Jan Marsh says, the implied metaphor, in a poem otherwise devoted to spring and the remembered promise of a fine lattermath, is that of mown meadows: "all flesh is grass, death the mower, scything men. These echoes connect the past and present green fields with the war and bring together the cutting of the hay and the infantry in battle."[22] Like 'As the team's head brass', this is a war poem and a fine one, too. Two of the greatest follow almost immediately, 'Bright clouds of may' and 'The long small room'. In the former, we see a pond half-shaded by may blossom, beyond:

All but one bay
Of emerald
Tall reeds
Like criss-cross bayonets
Where a bird once called,
Lies bright as the sun.

The mention of bayonets at once brings the war to mind and contributes to the atmosphere of ominous stillness in the poem. As in a vision, light and shadow contend, may blossom becoming "scum" in a vigorous rhyme with "blossom" which contradicts the fertile sense of the word and denies the appeal of spring. Instead we concentrate on the brilliant emerald reeds. In this suspension of time, everything catches breath while "Still the may falls", a natural process (like scum) which is quietly related to the dead hinted at by the metaphor of bayonets.

The setting of 'The long small room' is ingenious: a room in an old, dark house which narrows to one end. As the poet writes about it, he sees his right hand

> Crawling crab-like over the clean white page,
> Resting awhile each morning on the pillow,
> Then once more starting to crawl on towards age.
> The hundred last leaves stream upon the willow.

They "stream" because they are about to fall, an image which supports the idea of slow expiry in the preceding lines and is further impressed upon us by the traditional associations of willow and the unusual shape of the room. It is, we realise, that of a coffin.

These war poems were written by a soldier-poet contemplating the possibility of his extinction; the war is not the *subject* of the poems but the occasion for the expression of apprehensions which existed before it arose and which it brings to a head. The poetry serves not to reveal "war" — a subservience to subject noticeable in many war poets — but to define concerns that the war typifies but does not itself, except fortuitously, occasion. This is what happens when a poet looks at life under the aegis of battle: to describe a ploughman, a fallen elm, a dead oak, whispering aspens, betonies, reeds, a pond or willows is to see death everywhere. To think deeply, grievously, continuously of war leads to a retrospective of all one has known and to understandings only glimpsed at before. One sees what endures and learns to accept one's own mortality. One becomes inured to isolation and learns to convert familiar properties into poetic symbols, measuring one's language against perceptions in fresh words, simply and economically cadenced. For Thomas, the war was evidently not political or moral; and he could not have done justice to it if it were, but it offered him a view of life which dramatised his inner conflict and made him the war poet that he is.

The end was now near and he summoned up his energies to describe it. In 'The Green Roads', he tells of the ending of the road and the return to the forest in poignant terms, a goose-feathered track which marks the passage of one who is destined "never" to come back. All things "forget the forest" save himself, in the company of an old man and a child: youth and age. In 'When first I came here', hope "has gone for ever"; "the future and the maps/ Hide something I was waiting for". Since Thomas was employed as a map-reading instructor at the time, the allusion is clear: the army holds his destiny and the poem, his farewell to Steep, expresses his affection for his literary home, more evident "At parting than at meeting" (a characteristically ambivalent phrase). Yet if hope has gone, he is sure that love will grow, a love for "other hills" that is heavily circumscribed by the maps that secrete his desire. The "heart's dance" which attends his departure contains elements of both elation and anxiety, the joy of hope where none was said to exist and an undercurrent of fear lest it prove more obscure than he could wish.

'Blenheim Oranges' is poignant, too. The months drift by as rivers by "empty quays". It is raining, as "when the war began/ To turn young men to dung", a striking rhyme that prepares us for the image of a house standing "Outmoded, dignified,/ Dark and untenanted". This is evidently a self-portrait, recalling the "empty" of the second verse, as Thomas confesses: "I am something like that;/ Only I am not dead,/ Still breathing and interested/ In the house that is not dark:-". It is a brave effort but it is immediately countermanded by the last verse: "I am something like that:/ Not one pane to reflect the sun,/ For the schoolboys to throw at —/ They have broken every one." As Jan Marsh comments, "He was beginning to sign off: not yet dead, but withdrawing."[23]

The grim joy of 'The Trumpet' must have been one of the things Alun Lewis had in mind when he wrote about Thomas wanting death despite himself. The lovers who, in one way or another, have appeared in the poems as a locus of value finally disappear and the soldiers are urged on to "the old wars". In 'Lights Out', the poet once more stands on the brink of "The unfathomable deep/ Forest", the border of sleep "sweeter" than the noblest task. The human recoil is complete.

> There is not any book
> Or face of dearest look
> That I would not turn from now
> To go into the unknown
> I must enter, and leave, alone,
> I know not how.[24]

How "leave"? Was there, even now, hope against hope? Or is the forest darkness somehow converted into the entry to a freer life? "Only I want to come back more or less complete," Thomas told Frost.[25] Whatever the case, he listens to the silence and obeys it "That I may lose my way/ And myself."

It was, perhaps, the notion of the forest that called up the image of the path that ends "sudden"in Thomas's peripenultimate poem, 'Some day, I think...', delivering him finally to the dark in the beautifully sinister 'Out in the dark' where night finally overtakes the house it has been haunting so long and "all else is drowned". There is fear, naturally enough, but also stillness, the composure of one in the grip of an immeasurably greater force. This is the end of a long process, not the product of the emergency of Thomas's impending departure for France, and it throws light on all that has gone before. To be thus commanded is to be comforted. The tone is one of delicate enchantment before a horror so softened it has become seductive. In his last poem, 'The sorrow of true love', Thomas explains that the greatest sorrow derives from a less-than-perfect love since it has known neither the depths nor the heights, only "a frozen drizzle perpetual" of remorse and pity. A painful farewell.

The appreciation of the literature of World War I has been a matter as much of cultural as critical judgment and it is natural that the poet who best expressed such a bias should have received the greatest attention, assuring us that poetry is not where it is always and only to be found, in the poetry, but in the views and emotions it expresses — here, specifically, pity: "The Poetry is in the pity". Yet who can doubt at this distance in time that the bias needs correction and that Thomas's poetry is of a finer kind than Owen's? So long as we see him as the poet of the First World War, so long will we continue to misrepresent the literary history of the time. Needless to say, Thomas was not a poet of war in the same active sense, but it is no criterion of his standing as war poet that he should have served in the trenches any more than that Alun Lewis should have lived through the Japanese campaign in order to receive his acclaim as a poet of World War Two. To have known war as these poets knew it was to have knowledge of a different and particularly testing kind, one which illuminates war — and more than war — in ways that are not dependent on their having seen active service. As Lewis suggested in the material he provided for the cover for *Raiders' Dawn*, poets like him had "a completer understanding of the World War than could the poets of the 1914-18 War. Whereas men like Owen and Sassoon were severed from home by the continuous horror of the trench massacres he [i.e. Lewis] has been with the civilians in the bombed cities as well as with soldiers in their isolated camps....like Thomas the war has become an integral part of his life experience, not a violent thought-slaying wound as it was to Owen." It is a vital distinction and one which redefines the meaning of "war" in the twentieth century as a normative, civilian experience as well as a military one. Philip Larkin has put it this way:

> A "war poet" is not one who chooses to commemorate or celebrate a war, but one who reacts against having a war thrust upon him: he is chained, that is, to an historical event, and an abnormal one at that. However well he does it, however much we agree that the war happened and ought to be written about, there is still a tendency for us to withhold our highest praise on the grounds that a poet's choice of subject should seem an action, not a reaction. 'The Wreck of the Deutschland', we feel, would have been markedly inferior if Hopkins had been a survivor from the passenger list.[26]

Thomas and Lewis were all action.

NOTES

1. Lewis's *Horizon* review is reprinted in *Alun Lewis A Miscellany of His Writings* (Poetry Wales Press, 1982) pp.118-9.
2. *Keats* (Jack, 1916) p.72.
3. *Edward Thomas: A Portrait* R. George Thomas (Oxford University Press, 1985) p.188. See, too, *The Double*, Otto Rank, trans. and ed. by Harry Tucker, Jr., (University of North Carolina Press, 1971).
4. *ibid.*, p.102.
5. *ibid.*, p.103.
6. *Time and Again* Helen Thomas (Carcanet Press, 1978) p.74.
7. *Robert Frost: The Early Years 1874-1915* Lawrance Thompson (Holt, Rinehart & Winston, 1966) pp.463/4.
8. R. George Thomas, *op. cit.*, p.141-2.
9. *ibid.*, p.110.
10. *ibid.*, p.101.
11. *ibid.*, p.125.
12. *ibid.*, p.204.
13. *Keats*, p.73.
14. Quoted in *The Poetry of Edward Thomas* Andrew Motion (Routledge & Kegan Paul, 1980) p.88.
15. *ibid.*, p.65.
16. *ibid.*, p.92.
17. See, too, 'Inns and Books', *Horae Solitariae* (Duckworth, 1902) pp.39-40. The title essay sheds much light on Thomas's "moments of everlastingness".
18. See my 'Alun Lewis and Edward Thomas' *The Critical Quarterly*, 23,4,1982. pp.25-44.
19. *The Collected Poems of Edward Thomas* ed R. George Thomas (Oxford University Press, 1978) p.409.
20. For a fuller understanding of the figure in the door, see *The Happy-Go-Lucky Morgans* pp.233-9.
21. *Edward Thomas: A Poet for his Country* (Elek, 1978) p.178.
22. *ibid.*, p.174.
23. *ibid.*, p.177.
24. For the light Alun Lewis throws on this poem, see my *Alun Lewis: A Life* (Poetry Wales Press, 1984), pp.180-88.
25. *Edward Thomas: A Portrait, idem.*, p.284.
26. Quoted in Andrew Motion, *op.cit.*, pp.92-3.

JONATHAN BARKER

The Pocket Book of Poems and Songs for the Open Air:
Edward Thomas and the Folk Tradition

The Pocket Book of Poems and Songs for the Open Air: Edward Thomas and the Folk Tradition

In her essay ' "Worn New": Edward Thomas and English Tradition' (*Poetry in the Wars*, Bloodaxe Books, 1986), Edna Longley makes the point that "Yeats and Thomas shared the belief that folk song, in accordance with the Centaur view of culture, could provide powerful hindquarters for a complex literary art" and quotes part of Thomas's comment from *The South Country* (1909) "I prefer any country church or chapel to Winchester or Chichester or Canterbury Cathedral, just as I prefer 'All round my hat', or 'Sumer is icumen in', to Beethoven". 'All round my hat' is a traditional folk song and 'Sumer is icumen in' a round dating back to the thirteenth century. Both were included by Thomas with musical notation in his anthology *The Pocket Book of Poems and Songs for the Open Air* published by E. Grant Richards in 1907. R. George Thomas notes in *Letters from Edward Thomas to Gordon Bottomley* (1968) "ET's informed interest in folk-music illustrates the depth of his decision to live a country life and has almost passed unnoticed by critics of his poetry". R. George Thomas, Andrew Motion, and Edna Longley are exceptions, but the general critical neglect of the book has obscured from view that, as well as having a wide knowledge of literature (words consciously shaped for the printed page), Thomas was equally well acquainted with the folk tradition of narrative ballads, folk songs, nursery rhymes and carols which share a common root in music and dance. The two were living traditions to Thomas as Longley reminds us in her edition of *Poems and Last Poems* (1973) quoting from Thomas's *The Heart of England* (1906) on "the old ballads and folk songs and their airs":

> The words, in league with a fair melody, lend themselves to infinite interpretations, according to the listener's heart. What great literature by known authors enables us to interpret thus by virtue of its subtlety, ballads and their music force us to do by their simplicity. The melody and the story or the song move us suddenly and launch us into an unknown. They are not art, they come to us imploring a new lease of life on the sweet earth...

It is clear from this that Thomas felt deeply for the folk tradition, which he sees as naturally expressing man's most fundamental feelings and complementing the 'subtlety' of literature. The difficulty experienced by modern critics and historians in coming to terms with the folk tradition is quite simply the inability of we, whose medium is the written word, to stand outside that tradition and empathise with its older one time oral neighbour now long overtaken by apparent national literacy. What is more, the modern orthodoxy in literary criticism of 'the words on the page' discourages us from seeing much in a tradition in which the performance of words and music together communicates all at one hearing. Yet, as John Heath-Stubbs noted in *The Darkling Plain* (1950) the folk and literary traditions have influenced one another in the past:

> There is in English poetry, as in that of all other nations, a tradition of the folk, which lies behind, and is always influencing the great literary tradition. It manifests itself in May-day carol and harvest-song, in children's rhymes and dance-games, in ballads, humorous or moralizing — which often find their way into printed broad-sheets — in certain hymns and spontaneous expressions of piety, and, lastly, traditions in the rhymed epitaph. This folk-poetry has its roots in the old-fashioned village community, with its traditional occupations, and its seasonal rhythm of occasional holidays and festivals.

John Heath-Stubbs and David Wright represented the folk tradition alongside work by the recognised poets of the day in *The Forsaken Garden: An Anthology of Poetry 1824-1909* (1950), a technique introduced by Thomas Percy in his *Reliques of Ancient English Poetry* of 1765. Another anthology in the line is Edward Thomas's *The Pocket Book of Poems and Songs for the Open Air.* This was one of Thomas's earlier books: it was researched in his twenty-eighth year from July 1906 and was delivered to the publisher E. Grant Richards six months later for publication in 1907. The anthology contains a total of two hundred and thirty-four poems and songs of which sixty-one are acknowledged in the table of contents as 'Anonymous' poems, ballads, songs, or folk and sea songs; sixty songs, some by named authors, some not, include musical notation. The anthology is divided under thematic headings: The Invitation, The Start in the Morning, Wayside Rest, Village and Inn, The Footpath, Evening; and includes a surprising range of material in its three hundred and thirty-four pages: medieval songs, traditional ballads, sea shanties, folk songs, popular songs, drinking songs, an anonymous epitaph; and also poems, often on country themes, from Chaucer, Skelton, Spenser, Drayton, Shakespeare, Traherne, Herbert, Wordsworth, Keats, Shelley, Browning, Tennyson, Whitman etc., and contemporaries of Thomas's such as Belloc and W.H. Davies. Lyrics are included from, among others, Campion, Donne and Shakespeare (each with musical notation), with songs in French and Latin and translations from the Gaelic and Welsh, presumably by the compiler. Thomas in a letter to Gordon Bottomley of 11th November 1906 writes:

> A quarter of my anthology has gone to printers. The songs are glorious — You should hear Campion's 'White lope, blithe Helen & the rest', more religious than anything I know, & then 'Greensleeves' & 'Rio Grande' & Louis XIII's 'Amaryllis' & '*Orientis Partibus adventavit asinus*' (*La fête des fous*). It will be the best short collection in the world. I wish I thought as well of the poems.

Another letter to Bottomley of 9th December elaborates on this uncertainty over the poems:

> But in my endeavour to keep clear of what Lucas & other open air anthologists have used I daresay my poetry is not all good & not all popular enough & I shall not make £1,500 out of it as Lucas did out of his genial *Open Road* anthology.

This is a valid point: omissions from this anthology for the open air include Robert Burns and Robert Bloomfield, both poets with direct experience of country life and acquainted equally with literature and the folk tradition.

Thomas's excitement at the songs with musical notation and his insistence that Bottomley should *hear* the songs is a clear indication that they were intended to be sung as well as read on the page, presumably when holidaying in the countryside. This is implicit in the idea of a 'pocket book' which by definition is portable rather than scholarly, and for recreation rather than study. Thomas says in his 'Note by the Compiler':

> I have gathered into it much of the finest English poetry, and that poetry, at its best, can hardly avoid the open air. With this is some humbler poetry which is related to the finest as the grass to the stars: between the two I have often found it hard to choose. I have added about sixty of the sweetest songs which it seemed that a wise man would care to sing, or hear sung, in the fields, at the inn, on the road at dawn or nightfall, or at home.

This language is perhaps a bit arch (Bernard Bergonzi said it struck "the note of the hearty bookman") but it makes clear Thomas's sense of the two traditions — the subtlety of literature and simplicity of ballads — complementing rather than competing with one another. Thomas's contemporary G.K. Chesterton in his essay 'The Romance of Rhyme' (*The Mercury Book*, 1926) similarly notes "the true enjoyment of poetry is always in having the simple pleasure as well as the subtle pleasure" and adds that the "fatal metaphor of progress, which means leaving things behind us, has utterly obscured the real idea of growth, which means leaving things inside us".

Of what, then, does the folk tradition consist? On one level it is the whole world of folk lore and everything passed on orally from generation to generation for amusement or instruction without recourse to the written word, and instead relying on a tune ('air') or other mnemonic such as rhythm, rhyme or refrain. It incorporates poems as small as a nursery rhyme, as resonant and tragic as a ballad, and as simple in appeal to the emotions as a folk song. A.L. Lloyd in *Folk Song in England* (1975 edn.) points out, however, that printed broadside ballads and individual family song books existed for centuries, proving that the oral folk tradition was often complemented by written transmission as well. In fact the few aspects of the folk tradition to survive today partly on the oral level are children's games, lullabys and nursery rhymes: the latter called by Iona and Peter Opie "the true waifs of our literature", that "owe their present existence to this one quality of memorability". In them we meet a short verse line perhaps related to that found in late-Medieval literature as in the eighteenth century "Who killed Cock Robin?/ I, said the Sparrow,/ With my bow and arrow,/ I killed Cock Robin". Thomas acknowledges nursery rhyme in his poem 'The Child in the Orchard' where he asks "Who was the lady that rode the white horse/ With rings and bells to Banbury Cross?", and in 'The Penny Whistle':

> And her brother who hides apart in the thicket,
> Slowly and surely playing
> On a whistle an olden nursery melody,
> Says far more than I am saying.

Thomas's well documented innovations with the meditative conversational line relate him directly to literature at its most subtle and original; but many of his poems other than these internalised meditations of the Wordsworthian "fluxes and refluxes of the mind" show the influence of the folk tradition in their form in a way that has not been adequately acknowledged; chiefly because these poems are often of his second rank and not much discussed by critics. Evidence will be given later, but first we must turn back to *The Pocket Book of Poems and Songs for the Open Air* to trace both the development of the folk tradition and the occasions when that tradition and literature crossed paths as shown in Thomas's anthology. Among the oldest anonymous songs included are the medieval 'Sumer is icumen in', 'A New Year Carol', and the Elizabethan lyric beginning "Hey nonny no!/ Men are fools that wish to die!" written in a spare and at times irregular short line also present in John Skelton's "Merry Margaret/ As midsummer flower,/ Gentle as falcon/ Or hawk of the tower". Thomas Wyatt, another Tudor poet, is represented by part of his epistle 'To John Poins', but he in fact wrote in a wide variety of forms including the newly imported Italian sonnet and the short song line popular with courtiers and common folk alike. Examples are 'My Lute and I': "At moost mischief/ I suffre grief,/ For of relief/ Sins I have none", or the popular ditty "Ah, Robin,/ Jolly Robin,/ Tell me how thy leman doth/ And thou shall know of mine", a version of which Feste sings in *Twelfth Night*. Whether Wyatt adopted an existing song or his song joined the popular tradition is unclear: either way it suggests a two way traffic in Tudor days between literature and the song tradition, a view reinforced by

Shakespeare's use of song, for instance in *Hamlet* where both Ophelia and the gravedigger sing adaptations of folk songs, one in distraction, the other at work. *The Fitzwilliam Virginal Book*, a seventeenth century compilation of songs, includes folk songs together with songs by composers. Robert Herrick is another link from the seventeenth century between literature and song, in his adaptation of the short verse line in 'To Violets' alongside more complex verse forms. Moreover, from his Devonshire parish Herrick celebrated folklore ceremonies — "I sing of May-poles, Hock-carts, Wassails, Wakes" —, also 'Corinna's Maying', or the country harvest festival in 'The Hock-cart, or Harvest Home'.

As we move from the seventeenth into the eighteenth centuries (the former well, the latter badly represented in Thomas's anthology) we become involved in the development of the ballads, one specific line of the folk tradition represented in *The Pocket Book of Poems and Songs for the Open Air*. The ballads are narrative songs popular in both England and Scotland: some dating back to the Norman conquest, but most surviving from considerably later. The ballad stanza is a four line unit of alternating lengths of three and four feet, although considerable variations on this pattern exist. The metre is also found in hymns, which are again songs. Ballads are generally anonymous, narrative, dramatic, historical; they often adopt vivid imagery, and eschew moral comment. During the eighteenth century, the advent of cheap printing gave rise to a line of printed 'black letter' broadside ballads popular in town and country alike, extending their influence, however crudely, beyond the oral and into the printed word. However, it was not to these, but the older traditional oral ballads — such as 'The Ballad of Chevy-Chase' to which Sir Philip Sidney had far earlier paid tribute in his 'An Apologie for Poetrie' (1595):

> Certainly I must confesse my own barbarousnes, I never heard the olde song of *Percy* and *Duglas*, that I found not my heart mooved more then with a Trumpet: and yet is it sung but by some blinde Crouder, with no rougher voyce, then rude stile...

Both John Dryden and Samuel Pepys made collections of ballads for their own amusement, but the first major anthology is that compiled by Bishop Thomas Percy, and published in three volumes as *Reliques of Ancient English Poetry* in 1765.

Percy edited his book from a seventeenth century manuscript; he supplied extensive notes, a historical introduction and printed poets from the literary tradition alongside the ballads. One of these was William Shenstone who aided Percy in his pioneering work, and contributed 'Jemmy Dawson', a poem adapting the ballad form. *The Pocket Book of Poems and Songs for the Open Air* represents Shenstone by three pieces demonstrating his fusion of the simplicity of ballads with the subtlety of literature named by George Saintsbury "the artificial-natural style". 'The Village Schoolmistress' (shorn here from thirty-five to four stanzas) on the role of the school-teacher in village life and lore represents her as a figure near that of Thomas's 'Lob', the spirit of the folk tradition and folklore: "Herbs, too, she knew, and well of each could speak,/ That in her garden sipp'd the silv'ry dew". The tentative rhythmic movement of those lines is reminiscent of Thomas's "Women he liked, did shovel-bearded Bob", pointing out perhaps an unconscious similarity of approach between the two poets in blending the artificial and the natural.

Thomas represents a number of ballads in his anthology, including 'Sir Patrick Spens', and several Robin Hood ballads. He wrote on them in *The South Country*:

> I cannot help wondering whether the great work done in the last century and a half towards the recovery of old ballads in their integrity will have any effect beyond the entertainment of a few scientific men and lovers of what is ancient, now that the first effects upon Wordsworth and his contemporaries have died away. Can it possibly give a vigorous impulse to a new school of poetry that shall treat the life of our time and what in past times has most meaning for us as freshly as those ballads did the life of their time? It is possible; and it is surely impossible that such examples of simple, realistic narrative shall be quite in vain. Certainly the more they are read the more they will be respected, and not only because they often deal with heroic matters heroically, but because their style is commonly so beautiful, their pathos so natural, their observation of life so fresh, so fond of particular detail — its very lists of names being at times real poetry.

As Thomas points out Wordsworth was one poet to learn from the ballads through a desire to return poetry to simplicity of form and feeling and away from what he and Coleridge saw as the overelaborated expression of the Augustans. We see this both in the title of *Lyrical Ballads* (1798) and in his preface of 1802, where he claimed: "The earliest Poets of all nations generally wrote from passion excited by real events; they wrote naturally, and as men: feeling powerfully as they did". The daring and memorable plainness of the ballads regenerated Wordsworth's own poems, and their influence can clearly be seen in the form of early Romantic poems in Thomas's anthology: James Hogg's 'That's the Way', William Wordsworth's 'To the Cuckoo', John Keats's 'La Belle Dame Sans Merci', which consciously invents a new type of literary ballad; and less obtrusively in John Clare's 'Clare's Desire':

> Beside a runnel build my shed,
>   With stubbles cover'd o'er;
> Let broad oaks o'er its chimney spread,
>   And grass-plats grace the door.

John Clare as much if not more than Wordsworth manages to combine the conscious subtlety of literature with the natural rhythm of the folk tradition. Clare's father "could sing or recite above a hundred" ballads, so the poet was brought up hearing songs. In addition he later read ballads in printed form both as broadsides and in Percy's *Reliques*, of which he wrote to a correspondent: "I think it the most pleasing book I ever happend on the tales are familiar from childhood all the stories of my grandmother & her gossiping neighbours I find versified in these vols". Clare's involvement in the folk tradition is made clear in George Deacon's *John Clare and the Folk Tradition* (1983) which transcribes many of the songs the poet collected, along with tunes and even dance steps, in his native Northamptonshire.

Thomas Hardy, like Clare a poet from a musical family, adapted ballad metre in poems such as 'A Trampwoman's Tragedy' and 'The Darkling Thrush'. So did William Morris, John Davidson and A.E. Housman, each represented in Thomas's anthology by work which adapts and develops ballad form or mood. Andrew Motion in *The Poetry of Edward Thomas* (1980) comments on Thomas's use of "techniques usually associated with folk songs and ballads" in his poems. Edna Longley in her edition of *Poems and Last Poems* (1973) wrote that "The freshness of songs and ballads was a touchstone which helped Thomas to go back, like Frost, 'through the paraphernalia of poetry into poetry again' ". To what extent, then, might the ballad form have given "a vigorous impulse" to Thomas's own poems? First of all, 'The Penny Whistle', 'Home[1]', 'I built myself a house of glass', 'The Gallows', 'The Dark Forest' and many other poems are all written in a sensitive adaptation of ballad metre. In fact on close examination over one third of Thomas's one hundred and forty-four poems show evidence of the influence of the ballad tradition in adapting the four line ballad stanza pattern; occasionally but not often even retaining the alternate four and three foot line. Furthermore, the simplicity of the ballads is so skilfully assimilated into many Thomas poems, that it is a surprise on close examination to see the ghost of ballad metre still haunting, for instance, the understated rhythm of the second two lines quoted in 'Digging[1]':

> The smoke's smell, too,
> Flowing from where a bonfire burns
> The dead, the waste, the dangerous,
> And all to sweetness turns.

Before we turn from the plain grandeur of the ballads to the altogether subtler variations of personal emotion we find in southern English folk songs, we should first note that the short song line of Wyatt and other early poets represented in Thomas's anthology can also be found in his own poems. Their quick, fluid, natural movement makes these particular poems too easily taken for granted; they deserve more attention than they get from critics of Thomas. Examples are 'The Pond': "Bright clouds of may/ Shade half the pond./ Beyond,/ All but one bay"; "Will you come?/ Will you come?/

Will you ride/ So late/ At my side?/ O, will you come?"; 'Sowing': "And now, hark at the rain,/ Windless and light,/ Half a kiss, half a tear,/ Saying good-night"; 'Words': "Out of us all/ That make rhymes,/ Will you choose/ Sometimes —/ As the winds use/ A crack in a wall/ Or a drain" and also 'Under the Wood', 'The Thrush', 'Roads', '[M.E.T.]', 'After you Speak', 'Blenheim Oranges' all in varying degrees adapt the short song line and exploit its simplicity of cadence to good effect.

Folk songs are essentially the expression of a community: embracing work songs, lyrics, sea shanties, dance songs, carols, love songs and religious songs. Where the ballads are impersonal, folk songs are more often homely. They have a noticeably more relaxed freedom of rhythm, which adopts subtle lilting refrains in verse repeating stanzas. Their music is tuneful, melodically free; often in the older Dorian or Mixolydian modes with little harmony. Thomas's interest in folk song was recognised by Edna Longley in her essay 'Edward Thomas and the "English" Line' (*New Review*, February, 1975) wherein she links Thomas back to Wordsworth and Hardy and forward to Philip Larkin as a "missing link" in an alternative tradition to that of Eliot and Pound. Andrew Motion, in a 1982 *TLS* review of Ivor Gurney's *Collected Poems* extends the line to Gurney: "Gurney — like Thomas — secured and sustained a poetic line which was specifically English but nevertheless flexible and inclusive, at precisely the moment when the radical, cosmopolitan techniques of Pound and Eliot seemed to overwhelm it". David Wright argues from another connected viewpoint in his *Selected Poems and Prose* of Thomas in 1981:

> But Thomas's real place is last of the line of English poets who, beginning with Wordsworth, are not so much "nature" poets as recorders and elegizers of the slow destruction of rural England and its culture by the industrial revolution and its consequences. Thomas was well aware of the poems of his predecessors in that line — the then-forgotten John Clare and William Barnes, as well as of his older contemporary, Thomas Hardy.

The same editor, in his *Selected Poems of Thomas Hardy* (1978), links these regionalist poets to the folk tradition which he calls "a live traditional culture, the oral poetry of the people. It was a culture which in England survived almost unchanged from the Middle Ages up to the agricultural revolution and enclosure of the commons in the early nineteenth century and is now petrified in the collections of folk songs compiled by Cecil Sharp *et al*".

Evidence for this line of post-Wordsworthian regionalist poets acquainted with both the folk tradition and literature is present in Thomas's *The Pocket Book of Poems and Songs for the Open Air*. William Barnes, scholar, schoolmaster, philologist, musician, artist, priest, is included: he scarcely left his native Dorset, yet managed an inventiveness with lyric stanza forms barely matched in his day and surely an example to the young Thomas Hardy. John Clare, as we have seen, collected ballads and folk songs and also wrote original poems modelled on their forms. Clare vigorously defended the folk tradition while, like Thomas, in fact belonging more to conscious literature. As with Thomas, it is Clare's least inventive and original poems which exhibit most strongly the influence of folk songs. The depth of his feeling for them is expressed in a late poem, foreseeing the spirit of the folk song movement: "The Songs of our land are like ancient landmarks/ And curs'd be the traitor who takes one away". John Clare approaches greatness when he combines the natural lilt of folk song with the subtleties and modulations of literature as in: "Love lives beyond/ The tomb — the earth — which fades like dew/ I love the fond/ The faithfull & the true". But far and away the most distinguished poet in this line combining local knowledge of a folk tradition and printed literature is Thomas Hardy. As a boy he would dance to his father's violin tunes; and later played the violin with him at dances and festivals. Hardy's tireless experimentation with song stanza patterns, follows on from the example of William Barnes, but excels his master in range and theme: what is more, Hardy is able to breathe the spirit of folk song into literature — most impressively of all perhaps in 'During Wind and Rain':

> They sing their dearest songs —
> He, she, all of them — yea,
> Treble and tenor and bass,
>   And one to play;
> With the candles mooning each face....
>   Ah, no; the years O!
> How the sick leaves reel down in throngs!

Hardy also adapted actual folk songs into poems, 'Timing Her' is sub-titled '(Written to an old folk-tune)'; 'In the Small Hours' is on a dream in which he plays the viol tunes he played as a boy "Long reels and country-dances,/ And hornpipes swift and slow"; he even addresses a poem 'To my Father's Violin', and, two decades into our century, could claim unselfconsciously:

> Any little old song
>   Will do for me,
> Tell it of joys gone long,
>   Or joys to be,
> Or friendly faces best
>   Loved to see.

By the time Hardy published that poem in *Human Shows, Far Phantasies, Songs, and Trifles* (1925) the British folk song movement and the Folk Song Society were over twenty-five years old. The decline of folk song during the nineteenth century was directly related to the decline of the local village culture from which it grew: a decline linked to agricultural depression and the introduction of mechanised farming methods, improved transportation and, of course, industrialisation which created factory jobs in the larger towns. As individuals moved to the towns the songs they sang changed and developed to reflect an industrialised culture (incorporating the music hall, and songs of the labour movement), and naturally enough the traditional rural folk songs began to disappear. The Folk Song Society was part of an international local conservation movement intent on writing down the words and tunes of songs, often directly from the lips of singers. The process began too late to save a multitude of local material which relied on oral transmission, but it did preserve a good number: others had already been transcribed into written form by members of the local community or enthusiasts years before. The preservation of songs in transcribed form changed them irrevocably from entertainment for a local culture into a consciously studied art form, a precious part of our popular heritage. Curiously the act of transcribing what had been a constantly modifying pattern of words and tune from the voice to the written page, and the melodies from the Dorian mode to the treble clef, immediately and irrevocably translated the words once and for all out of the remains of the folk tradition and into that of literature. A further irony is that the increasing middle class audience of readers and consumers of literature (created by the very process which signalled the end of the folk tradition) were to be the audience for the songs in their new context of literary cultural nostalgia.

Prominent in the British folk song movement were the Rev. Sabine Baring-Gould, Rev. John Broadwood, Miss Lucy Broadwood, Frank Kidson, Rev. C.L. Marson, Ralph Vaughan Williams and, more than any other, Cecil Sharp, who collected almost five thousand songs and tunes: his *Folk Songs from Somerset* was published between 1904-1909. James Reeves provides an amusing picture of the collecting and transcribing process in *The Idiom of the People* (1958) where he tells how in 1903 Cecil Sharp and C.L. Marson at Hambridge, Somerset took down 'The Seeds of Love' "from the lips of the vicar's own gardener, a man with the remarkably symbolic name of John England". Sharp harmonized the song, and that evening it was sung at a choir supper. One of the local audience is reported to have said later that it was "the first time that the song had been put into evening-dress". Edward Thomas's *The Pocket Book of Poems and Songs for the Open Air*, compiled in 1906 and published in 1907 can, in this context, be seen as part of the folk song movement. R. George Thomas's edition of the *Letters from Edward Thomas to Gordon Bottomley* (1968) reveals Thomas as collector of folk songs both from contemporary printed and oral sources: "I have 3 jolly unpublished sailors' songs for the Anthology". So does his 'Note by the Compiler' in the anthology, where he mentions songs discovered at a Westmorland festival:

> These Westmorland songs have, I think, never been published before, except two of them in a book called *The Heart of England* [also edited by Thomas and published in 1906]. 'The Mowing Song', 'The Whale', 'Salt Beef', and 'The Princess Royal' are also from an oral source. Some of the

> combinations of airs and words are Mr. Freeman's and mine, viz. 'Meum est Propositum', 'Marching Along', and 'Three Men of Gotham'.

This shows a pretty creative involvement with the folk tradition, both as collector of songs and in fitting the words to a tune. A letter to Bottomley of 9th December 1906 informs us that Thomas fitted existing tunes to Thomas Love Peacock's 'Three Men of Gotham' and Robert Browning's 'Kentish Sir Byng'; and we also find that Thomas had contact with Cecil Sharp in his explanation why he prints two separate tunes, one major, one minor, with the sea song 'Spanish Ladies':

> And I will add Masefield's version, but must retain that in the minor. Cecil Sharp (who knows) says no *old* sailor would sing the major tune that Masefield gives, & it was he who gave me the version I am using. It is not obvious but I have learned to like it well. 'All round my hat' is obviously from B-Gould, because verse 3 is almost entirely the work of his collaborator (Fleetwood Sheppard): so he must have his guinea.

Thomas had probably learnt to like Sharp's minor tune through singing it. (R. George Thomas in his *Edward Thomas: A Portrait* (1985) provides plentiful evidence of Thomas's "good singing voice and love of songs".) Fleetwood Sheppard's additions to 'All Round my Hat' remind us that the act of 'transcribing' a song can result in altering the words. The possible motives stretch from prudery, attempts to 'improve' the words, or adapt them for a school audience, to even the mundane mishearing or forgetting of lines during transcription. The frankness of some songs, bypassing the sexual restraint of much love poetry, at times led to verses being altered or dropped. Thomas for instance includes in his anthology a version of 'A-begging we will go' which is far tamer than one earlier transcribed by John Clare in Northamptonshire. Thomas also includes in his anthology 'Blow away the Morning Dew' and 'Dabbling in the Dew' from *Folk Songs from Somerset* edited by Cecil Sharp and Charles L. Marson, and 'The Cheerful Horn' from *English Country Songs* edited by Lucy Broadwood and J.A. Fuller Maitland. 'Waly, Waly', is included, as is 'Men are Fools that wish to Die' which he probably found in A.H. Bullen's influential *Lyrics from the Song-Books of the Elizabethan Age* (1889).

In its small way Thomas's anthology places him firmly within the folk song movement. It also represented the qualities of the folk tradition to readers of literature at a time when poetry was in the doldrums. Leading established poets of the day — William Watson, Robert Bridges and Laurence Hope — were all masters of a superb unnaturalness of diction and phrase. The movement had creative results. Just as we earlier saw that the ballads reinvigorated literature through their influence on Wordsworth and the Romantics, so a century later the rediscovery of folk song music was, in Thomas's words, to give "a vigorous impulse to a new school". This time it was one of composers and songwriters including Charles Stanford, Percy Grainger, Frederick Delius, and especially Ralph Vaughan Williams who himself collected over eight hundred folk songs and whose allied interest in Tudor and folk music influenced Herbert Howells, Ivor Gurney, Gerald Finzi — a line continued in Benjamin Britten's settings of folk songs. Of these names surely the nearest in spirit to Thomas is Ivor Gurney, a man equally distinguished as poet and songwriter, and who set a sequence of Thomas's poems (titled 'Lights Out') to music between 1918-1925. He revered Thomas's poems and shared a feeling for the names of things and places, combining this with a Hopkinsian empathy for what Gurney called "The dearness of common things,/ Beech wood, tea, plate shelves,/ And the whole family of crockery,/ Woodaxes, blades, helves". In Michael Hurd's biography *The Ordeal of Ivor Gurney* (1978) Helen Thomas is quoted writing about a visit made with Marion Scott to Gurney in Dartford Asylum when she and Gurney, on Edward's ordnance maps, retraced the lanes of Gloucester once walked by both poets at different times. Gurney only set one of his own poems to music: in it his sometimes knotty, intense style is replaced by an equally characteristic lucidity, at times reminiscent of Thomas:

> Only the wanderer
>   Knows England's graces,
> Or can anew see clear
>   Familiar faces...

Edward Thomas's own poems contain various specific elements belonging to the folk song tradition. 'The Gypsy' for instance includes a scene of a Gypsy entertaining workmen with tambourine and mouth-organ with 'Over the hills and far away'. Elsewhere Thomas perhaps followed Dante Gabriel Rossetti's example from 'An Old Song Ended' in integrating parts of folk songs in his two poems titled 'An Old Song', numbered by R. George Thomas as [1] and [2]. The first is an adaptation of 'The Lincolnshire Poacher', a song included in both *The Pocket Book of Poems and Songs for the Open Air* and later in *This England: An Anthology from her Writers* (Oxford University Press, 1915) along with a number of other folk songs and ballads. The final stanza of both the folk song and Thomas's adaptation follows:

> Success to every gentleman that lives in Lincolnshire,
> Success to every poacher that wants to sell a hare,
> Bad luck to every gamekeeper that will not sell his deer.
>   Oh, 'tis my delight on a shining night in the season of the year!
> (Traditional)
>
> And with this melody on my lips and no one by to care,
> Indoors, or out on shiny nights or dark in open air,
> I am for a moment made a man that sings out of his heart:
>   Oh, 'tis my delight of a shiny night in the season of the year. (Thomas)

'An Old Song [2]' incorporates the refrain (already previously used by Byron in his 'So we'll go no more a roving' in 1817), "I'll go no more a-roving/ With you, fair maid" from the sea-shanty 'A-Rovin', into his poem as the final two lines.

Thomas titled three of his poems 'Song', numbered [1], [2], [3] respectively by R. George Thomas. Of 'Song [3]', R. George Thomas notes that Thomas wrote to Eleanor Farjeon "I am sending you a sober set of verses to the tune of Rio Grande, but I doubt if they can be sung. Are they worth copying?". 'Rio Grande' is included in *The Pocket Book of Poems and Songs for the Open Air* as a 'sea song'. Thomas's own poem continues the considerable gusto of the original, before ending more plaintively:

> The past is the only dead thing that smells sweet,
> The only sweet thing that is not also fleet.
> I'm bound away for ever,
> Away somewhere, away for ever.

The note was not new to literature; Alfred Tennyson, haunted lifelong by the words "Far-far-away" — possibly a variation on 'Over the hills and far away' — eventually towards the end of his life wrote a poem of that title for music. Thomas's adaptations of folk songs into his own early poems provide direct evidence for his knowledge of the folk tradition and his desire to learn from it; as we saw earlier in 'The Penny Whistle' where "an olden nursery melody,/ Says far more than I am saying".

That "olden"sums up the essentially backward-looking nature of the folk tradition; usually referring back, with subtle variations, to a well-tested verse form or simple and memorable air inherited not invented, and expressing continuities of place, spirit and feeling. The concept of the "olden" appears throughout Thomas's poems: for instance, the "This England, Old already" of 'The Manor Farm'; the "old inhabitant of earth" of 'The Other'; the "feathery herb", 'Old Man'; the badger that "most ancient Briton of English beasts" of 'The Combe'; the "Older than Clare and Cowper, Morland and Crome" of 'Haymaking'; and the "old man's face, by life and weather cut", "old Jack" of 'Lob', the archetype of man in touch with the folk tradition.

The simpler poems of Edward Thomas examined here are a thread linking him to a 'line' I have traced via the poems of *The Pocket Book of Poems and Songs for the Open Air* through Hardy, Clare, Barnes, Wordsworth, Shenstone, Percy's *Reliques*, Shakespeare's songs, to Skelton and Wyatt in whom we glimpse a (now impossible) shared awareness of both literature and the folk as living traditions enlivening and adding to one another by turns.

SELECT BIBLIOGRAPHY

Edward Thomas: *The Pocket Book of Poems and Songs for the Open Air* (Grant Richards) 1907.
Edward Thomas: *This England: An Anthology from her Writers* (Oxford University Press) 1915.
Thomas Percy: *Reliques of Ancient English Poetry: Consisting of Old Heroic Ballads, Songs, and Other Pieces of Our Earlier Poets Together With Some Few of Later Date* 1765 3 vols.
George Deacon ed. *John Clare and the Folk Tradition* (Sinclair Browne) 1983
Walter Scott: *Minstrelsy of the Scottish Border* ed. with a new glossary, Thomas Henderson (Harrap) 1931
Francis James Child: *The English and Scottish Popular Ballads* (Dover) 1965 5 vols.
Bertrand Harris Bronson: *The Traditional Tunes of the Child Ballads* (Princeton University Press) 1959-72 4 vols.
William Allingham: *The Ballad Book* (Macmillan) 1879.
W.H.Auden & John Garrett: *The Poet's Tongue* (G.Bell) 1935.
John Heath-Stubbs & David Wright: *The Forsaken Garden* (Lehmann) 1950.
Matthew Hodgart: *The Faber Book of Ballads* (Faber) 1965.
Geoffrey Grigson: *The Penguin Book of Ballads* (Penguin) 1975.
V de Sola Pinto & A.E. Rodway: *The Common Muse* (Chatto & Windus) 1957.
Robert Graves: *English and Scottish Ballads* (Heinemann) 1957.
Matthew Hodgart: *The Ballads* (Hutchinson) 1962.
Albert B. Friedman: *The Ballad Revival* (University of Chicago Press) 1961.
David Buchan: *The Ballad and the Folk* (Routledge & Kegan Paul) 1972.
Lucy Broadwood & J.A. Fuller Maitland: *English Country Songs* (Leadenhall P.) 1893.
S.Baring-Gould & H. Fleetwood Sheppard: *A Garland of Country Song* (Methuen) 1895.
Cecil James Sharp & C.L. Marson: *Folk Songs from Somerset* (Wessex Press) 1904-09.
William Chappell: *Popular Music of the Olden Time* (Dover Pubns.) 1965 2 vols.
Cecil James Sharp: *English Folk Song: Some Conclusions* (Methuen) 1954.
Cecil James Sharp: *Collection of English Folk Songs* (Oxford University Press) 1974 2 vols.
A.L. Lloyd: *Folk Song in England* (Paladin) 1975
Ralph Vaughan Williams & A.L. Lloyd: *The Penguin Book of English Folk Songs* (Penguin) 1959.
Roy Palmer: *Folk Songs Collected by Ralph Vaughan Williams* (Dent) 1983.
James Reeves: *The Idiom of the People* (Heinemann) 1958.
James Reeves: *The Everlasting Circle* (Heinemann) 1960.
Iona & Peter Opie: *The Oxford Dictionary of Nursery Rhymes* (Oxford University Press) 1951.
Iona & Peter Opie: *The Puffin Book of Nursery Rhymes* (Penguin) 1963.
R.T. Davies: *Medieval English Lyrics* (Faber) 1963.
Bruce Pattison: *Music and Poetry of the English Renaissance* (Methuen) 1948.
John Heath-Stubbs: *The Darkling Plain* (Eyre & Spottiswoode) 1950.
Victor E. Neuburg: *Popular Literature* (Penguin) 1977.
Edna Longley: *Poetry in the Wars* (Bloodaxe Books) 1986.

Index of the Works Discussed

Title index of writings (including poems, essays, stories, books, but excluding reviews) by Thomas discussed. No critical or biographical works on Thomas are included. Titles to poems follow those of R. George Thomas's edition of the poems. In a few cases a title here refers back to the first line of a poem. 'n' = note.

Notes on Contributors

Peter Levi is Professor of Poetry at Oxford. His recent publications include *Shakespeare's Birthday* (Anvil), *The Flutes of Autumn* (Harvill) and *The Pelican History of Greek Literature*. He is presently writing a life of Shakespeare.

John Bayley is Warton Professor of English and a Fellow of St. Catharine's, Oxford. He has written books on Pushkin, Tolstoy, Hardy and Shakespeare, and is the author of *The Characters of Love* and *The Romantic Survival*. Married to Iris Murdoch, his novel *In Another Country* recently appeared in paperback.

J.P. Ward is a lecturer in the Department of English, University College, Swansea. An admired poet and critic his most recent volume of verse was *The Clearing* (Poetry Wales Press, 1984). He has written on Wordsworth, Raymond Williams, and *Poetry and the Sociological Idea*, and his *The Poetry of R.S. Thomas* will appear in 1987.

Robert Wells is a poet and freelance writer. His publications include *The Winter's Task* (1977), a verse translation of Virgil's *Georgics* (Carcanet, 1982), *Selected Poems* (Carcanet, 1986) and a verse translation of Theocritus's *Idylls* (Carcanet, Forthcoming).

Sally Roberts Jones's most recent collection of poetry was *Relative Values* (Poetry Wales Press, 1984). A librarian by training, she runs her own publishing company, Alun Books, in south Wales.

Jeremy Hooker is a freelance writer and poet. His poetry collections include *Solent Shore* (Carcanet, 1978) and *Englishman's Road* (1980), and he is the author of a book of essays, *Poetry of Place* (1982). A new collection of essays, *The Presence of the Past* (Poetry Wales Press) will appear in 1987.

Dick Davis is a full time writer, who has had three collections of poetry published by Anvil. His reviews and articles appear in the leading U.K. journals, and his full length study of Yvor Winters was published in America in 1983.

John Pikoulis is a Senior Lecturer in the Department of Extra-Mural Studies, University College, Cardiff. He is the author of *The Art of William Faulkner*, and of the biography *Alun Lewis: A Life* (Poetry Wales Press, 1984).

Jonathan Barker is the Librarian at the Arts Council's Poetry Library in London. He edited the *Selected Poems of W.H. Davies* (Oxford University Press, 1985) and the *Poetry Book Society Anthology 1986-87* (Hutchinson, 1986).